"I'M ASKING YOU NICELY"

About the author

Greg Watts is a freelance journalist and author. He has written for numerous publications, including *The Times*, *The Guardian* and the *Evening Standard*, as well as working in TV and radio. He lives in London.

By the same author:

Don't Drop the Coffin *(Hodder and Stoughton)*
Meeting the Guv'nor *(Hodder and Stoughton)*
From Gangland to Promised Land *(xt3 Ltd)*
Released: Stories from Prison to Faith and Hope *(Alive Publishing)*

Some of the names and places have been changed.

About Highland Books

Find out more about us and our other publications on our website: www.highlandbks.com
If you see a mistake you can e-mail us at errata@highlandbks.com
Book-specific page:
http://i1897913753.highlandbks.net

"I'M ASKING YOU NICELY"

The Es Kaitell biography

Greg Watts

Highland Books

Godalming, Surrey

First published in 2005 by Highland Books,
Two High Pines, Knoll Road, Godalming, Surrey GU7 2EP.

ISBN 1-897913-75-3

Cover photos by Saxon Bashford

Book design and production for the publisher by
Bookprint Creative Services, P.O. Box 827, BN21 3YJ, England.
Printed in Great Britain.

Contents

Chapter One

No Tools

Es Kaitell's voice tightened, "You have probably heard that I became a Christian a few months ago . . . from now on we're going to do the job differently."

Black, well-built and a towering 6' 5", Es Kaitell was well known in and around east London. His security firm, set up seven years earlier, ran the doors at some of the roughest pubs and clubs in the area. He was addressing forty of his doormen, who were sitting in rows in the room of what had been Crews nightclub at Fairlop Waters, near Barkingside, one Monday evening. He hadn't told them over the phone what the meeting was to be about, but he had stressed that it was very important that they all turned up.

They all stared back blankly.

"We're going to lay down our weapons, we're going to wear uniforms, we're going to polish our shoes, clean our fingernails, and we're going to meet and greet. We're going to treat people with respect," continued Es.

He could tell from the looks on the guys' faces that they thought he had lost the plot. Asking them to go to work without their tools was like asking them to go to work without their clothes on. In security, tools such as knuckledusters, coshes, knives and baseball bats were considered an integral part of the job. He knew that he was taking a huge risk. They might all decide to leave and go and work for someone else.

"And I'm going to start a training school," he continued. "Has anyone got any questions?"

The guys just sat there, looking shocked. No one said anything. Several of them then stood up and made their way towards the door, while others began talking in huddles.

"Es, how are we meant to do our job without tools? It's impossible," asked a barrel-chested guy who had only been with Es for a few weeks.

"It's not impossible, mate. Nothing's impossible if God's with you."

The guy shook his head. "I don't think you can do it."

"So what are you saying? We take a Bible instead of a duster?" said another doorman sarcastically.

"Trust me. We can do it," replied Es.

"So what would have happened the other week at that pub in north London if we hadn't've had dusters?" he retorted. A dozen Turkish guys had attacked five doormen the previous Saturday night. Had they not been tooled up with coshes and dusters, they would have been beaten to a pulp – just like he had been that night at the Ilford Palais a few months before.

Deep down, Es too wondered if it was possible. How were his guys meant to deal with punters who came tooled up if they only had their hands to defend themselves? Wasn't he putting them at risk? Maybe it wasn't compatible to work the doors and also be a Christian. He knew that he had to place his faith in God.

Es with his adopted father, at home in Dagenham.

A staunch Hammer!

Chapter Two

The Outsider

Growing up as a black child with white adopted parents was almost unheard of in England in the 1960s. And in Dagenham, where Es grew up, there were very few black faces to be seen in the streets. Back then, black people in the London area tended to live in Brixton, Notting Hill and Harlesden.

Es's biological parents came from Sierra Leone in West Africa, from families of well-to-do professionals. His father came to London to study civil engineering and his mother to study midwifery. Things didn't work out between them, though, and they ended up getting divorced.

After Es was born at St Mary's Hospital, Paddington, west London, in 1959 he was placed in a foster home. When he was eighteen months old he and his five-year-old brother Merrill were adopted by a middle-aged East End couple, Lily and George Warner, whom Es regarded as his parents. They already had two children of their own, twenty-four-year-old Jill, who was more or less living away from home, and nineteen-year-old Gerald, and they had also already adopted Es's sister, Yvonne, who was five years older than him, after replying to an advert in a newspaper.

The Warners lived in a terraced two up, two down in Fitzstephen Road, Dagenham. While the house was simply furnished, the back garden was full of geraniums, roses, candytuft and fruit trees, along with baby animal ornaments and garden gnomes.

Situated on the edge of London, but technically in Essex, Dagenham was a bleak, mainly white, working-class area with many of the population employed at the sprawling Ford's car factory, which stretched all the way from the A13 down to the River Thames.

Es's dad worked as a beveller for a glass company near Tower Bridge. He came from a large family in West Ham. Because he had splayed feet, he'd failed his medical for the army during the Second World War and instead was given a job in the civil defence. Like many of his generation, he was a hard-working, principled, conscientious man who would never owe anyone a penny. He was the chairman of the Glass Workers' Union and one of the founder members of the Dagenham Labour Party. Although he didn't earn a lot of money, the family was always well provided for. One of the rare luxuries he allowed himself was a few ounces of St Julian tobacco for his pipe and roll-ups.

Mum also came from a big family, in Plaistow. Because her hair had gone white early on, she had dyed it blue. Although money was tight, she loved to have the occasional flutter on the horses, dogs or an important West Ham United game. Es would sometimes find her Coral betting slips and pencils around the house.

Es didn't think there was anything unusual about growing up with white parents until he went to Roding Junior School, where he was the only black pupil. At break one morning a group of children crowded round him and one of them said, "Hello, monkey." The others burst into a fit of giggles.

"What do you mean, monkey? I ain't a monkey," replied Es, his lips trembling.

The kids began laughing at him, singing, "Monkey! Monkey! Monkey!"

"I ain't a monkey," repeated Es. "Stop it!"

"You belong in the zoo 'cos you're a monkey," taunted a boy with pixie eyes and freckles.

Es stood there, watching them as they skipped across the playground still singing. He could feel his eyes welling up with tears. Why were they picking on him? What had he done? What made him different? These feelings were compounded each morning and afternoon when the parents waiting at the school gates would stare at him and his mum. He couldn't understand why they did this. He felt that he wanted to be invisible.

But at home he was very happy. He used to go with Merrill and his friends to Mayesbrook Park and Parsloes Park, where they would play football, boxing, using jumpers as a ring, cricket, or build go-karts from pram wheels and bits of wood, or tree houses. They also made Dutch arrows, which involved cutting a piece of a cane at one end and then attaching flights made from cornflakes packets and a piece of string. There was an area of the park with a clump of trees, and he used to find it exciting when he wandered in there. With his pocket money, he would buy pop and crisps from a shop next to Becontree station.

Es's parents rarely went out in the evening; instead they would watch TV or play cards with the children for matchsticks. They both loved music. His dad would often play his violin and his mum the piano, and they enjoyed listening to Gilbert and Sullivan and the Proms. His mum enjoyed reciting lines from Shakespeare – something she had picked up from her father, who could recite the plays by heart. Es used to look forward to Friday evenings when his dad, wearing his trilby hat and carrying his silver-handled cane, would bring him sweets and *Beano* and *Dandy* comics. He used to enjoy reading about the antics of the Bash Street Kids, Denis the Menace and Keyhole Kate.

At Christmas, all his aunties and uncles would come around laden with presents. His dad would pluck and clean the turkey, cook it overnight and then, on Christmas day, put on a white apron and chef's hat and carve it on the kitchen table. He was renowned for his pork and sage and onion stuffing. In the evenings they would all gather in the living room and have a sing-song.

When Es was seven, his dad took him for the first time to Upton Park, to see West Ham United play Manchester United. He was thrilled by the electric atmosphere at the ground, and he felt proud when his dad lifted him high over the heads of the crowd on the terrace and down to the front, so that he could get a better view.

As was the case for most families in Dagenham, long holidays were out of the question, so instead they took the train for days out in Southend-on-Sea. They would always get off at Leigh-on-Sea station and walk the rest of the way along the coast, passing the cockle sheds and stopping off at the Smack Inn for lemonade. Es used to love paddling in the sea, playing cricket on the beach and going on the rides on Southend pier.

At the age of eight he started going with his mates to judo classes at Kingsley Hall at Martin's Corner. He enjoyed it and found that he was good at it.

Dad was never happier than when he was pottering about in a small shed at the bottom of the garden. Es used to stand in the corner watching fascinated as, whistling loudly, his dad expertly lathed, chiselled and sawed pieces of wood to produce a table or chair. Es could see how contented he was.

Es came home from school one afternoon to find an ambulance pulling away from outside his house. He rushed into the living room to find his mum sitting on the settee, crying.

"What's up, Mum?" he asked, worried.

She looked up at him, dabbing her eyes with a handkerchief. "It's your dad."

"What's the matter with him?"

"He's been taken to hospital, son. But don't worry, he's going to be all right."

In fact, his dad had suffered a serious heart attack. He returned home a couple of weeks later, but his weak condition forced him to give up work, and money became tighter. Nevertheless, his dad made sure he could still buy Es his comics and sherbet lemons from the sweet shop at Martin's Corner.

Es used to stay with his biological mother occasionally at her large house in West Hampstead but, for some reason, he always felt strange when he was there. On Sunday mornings he used to sit at a table in the dark cellar and eat ice cream for breakfast, which struck him as odd. He would then put on his Sunday best clothes and go with his mother to a big old church. When they went in, she would hand him a black hymnbook and then take a seat near the front. He tried to join in the singing, but it sounded dreary and he didn't understand the words. He couldn't wait to get back to Dagenham. He didn't want to be in West Hampstead, his mother seemed distant and stern, and there was something about the house and atmosphere that felt cold.

"Mum, where is Sierra Leone?" asked Es one day after returning from a weekend in West Hampstead.

"It's in Africa. A long way away," she replied, smiling at his question.

"What's it like there?"

"I don't know, Es. I think it's probably very hot. It wouldn't be like here."

Es used to lie awake at night thinking about Sierra Leone, wondering how different from Dagenham it was. One day, he took down his dad's battered atlas from the shelf in the living room and flicked through the pages until he found Africa. Staring at the map, he thought how small Sierra Leone looked. It was tiny. Maybe he would go there one day when he was a grown-up.

When he was eleven, he left Roding Junior school and went to Erkenwald Secondary School. Apart from English and sport, he didn't really excel at his studies, although he tried hard. However, he made it into the school's football, cricket, basketball and athletic teams. Mr Orton, who taught PE, gave Es a lot of encouragement. "Good lad, keep it up. You've got the makings of a champ if you stick at it," he would often say to him in the changing room. Football was Es's real passion. His dad bought him his first pair of football boots from Cross's sports shop in Barking and he joined Vallance United, who played in a Sunday league on a pitch at Vallance Park. Es began as a left winger, because he was fast, and then switched to sweeper. He used to imagine that he was his hero Bobby Moore, who played in the same position. When the manager of the team held a competition to design a new kit and he won it with his design of blue shorts and a blue top with a yellow V, he was elated.

It was unusual for Es to see any other black people. This only occurred on the rare occasion when he left Dagenham and went on a school trip to a museum in central London or travelled on the Underground to his adopted sister Jill's house in Wembley Park. Jill's husband was Indian, and they had got married in a Hindu ceremony. When Es did see another black person, he didn't feel quite so different. And although he supported England when they played the West Indies at cricket, he liked to see black players such as Gary Sobers or Clive Lloyd doing well. He felt inspired by them. He had become aware that in some parts of the world black people were treated badly. On TV he had watched scenes of race riots in Alabama, USA, where Dr Martin Luther King had called for non-violent protest, and he had also seen black people in South Africa being fired at by the police and army. He couldn't understand why this was happening.

Gary Slade, who had the reputation for being the best fighter in the school, began picking on him, but one day Es decided to stand up to him. After school, they squared up to each other on a piece of nearby waste ground, watched by a dozen other lads."Come on, then," challenged Slade. "Hit me!"

His heart pumping, Es aimed a punch at him. But Slade moved sideways and it missed. Slade then grabbed him round the neck, wrestled him to the floor and began punching his face. Es tried to push him off, but he was too strong.

"Give in?"

"Yeah," cried Es, wriggling furiously to get free. "I give in."

But he was determined to stand up to Slade, so the following week they had another fight. Slade won again, but after this he didn't pick on him. Es felt that he had earned Slade's respect.

He never bunked off school, like some of his mates, and he hardly ever got into fights, apart from the time he took on Gary Slade. He plodded along through his school years. The only thing that set him apart was the fact that he was black. Mr Bird said to him one day in class, "Do you blush, Esmond?" He didn't know what to say. How could he ask something like this? He wanted to say, "Just because I have black skin doesn't mean that I don't have blood running through my veins." But he felt too shy to do so.

When he was twelve, his biological mother turned up at the house one afternoon, looking very serious.

"I'm planning to take Esmond to America," she said firmly, stepping into the hallway. "I'm going to live in Ohio."

"You are?" replied Es's mum, shooting a glance at a nervous-looking Es beside her.

"Yes, I am."

"I see," she said calmly.

"You'll be hearing from me." And with that, his biological mother turned and walked out.

After she had left, Es said to his mum, "I don't want to go to America. I'm happy here. And Yvonne and Merrill are with me." He had tears in his eyes.

She hugged him close and said soothingly, patting his head, "Don't worry, love. We're not going to let anyone take you away. We'll fight them all the way and we'll go to court if we have to. This is your home."

Despite her reassurances, Es lived in constant fear of being taken away. He knew that Lily and George were only his adopted parents.

During the summer holidays he worked in a travel agent's on Oxford Street run by Jill's husband. One of Es's jobs was to deliver airline tickets to various offices. He found the West End fascinating. Unlike Dagenham, there were old buildings, enormous department stores, theatres, fancy restaurants and hotels. There was a real buzz in the air. And as he walked through the crowded streets or travelled on the Underground and buses, he saw people of every kind of skin colour and heard dozens of different languages.

"So, Es, what do you think you want to do when you leave school?" asked his dad one Saturday evening while they waited for *Match of the Day* to come on TV.

Es shrugged. "I don't know, Dad."

"No? Oh well, you've still time to decide. But remember, the important thing in life is to keep an open mind and to try to do your best."

Es thought a lot about his dad's question. What did he want to do? Then one afternoon when he was kicking a ball around in the back garden it came to him. He would be a bodyguard, like those men in dark suits he had seen on TV guarding the royal family. He liked the idea of protecting people, and it seemed a mysterious and glamorous job.

He left school in the summer of 1975. When the exam results came out he got a grade 1 CSE in English language and also CSEs in history, woodwork, metalwork, maths and geography. He was still unsure of what he wanted to do. Around this time, he saw an advertisement in the *Evening Standard* for the Metropolitan Police and decided to apply. He'd never really thought much about the police, but the idea of helping people appealed to him. He still wanted to be a bodyguard, but he hadn't seen any adverts for them.

"Dad, I'm thinking of joining the police," said Es one day at tea.

"The police?" replied his dad, raising his eyebrow and putting down his copy of the *Daily Mirror*.

"Yeah, I've seen a newspaper advert."

"I see. Well, son, if that's what you want to do," he said. But Es could see from his dad's face that he didn't seem very enthusiastic at the prospect of his son becoming a policeman.

A few weeks later, on a grey, miserable day, Es was sitting in a packed carriage on a Northern Line train on his way to the police training college at Hendon for an open day. He felt nervous and a bit silly that he thought himself good enough to join the police.

The rain was sleeting down when he arrived at the college. A policeman with a thick moustache directed him to the canteen and told him to wait there until his name was called. He felt very self-conscious sitting in the large canteen, sipping his mug of undrinkable coffee. Glancing around, he noticed that a number of police cadets were giving him curious looks. 'I don't belong here,' he thought to himself, and got up and walked out.

Having dismissed the idea of the police, Es decided to become a painter and decorator, and he was accepted for a three-year apprenticeship with the London Borough of Barking and Dagenham, which included day and block release at East Ham College, to study for a City and Guilds certificate. He enjoyed the work and the banter he had with the other guys. Seeing that he was good at the job, he became more confident. He passed his apprenticeship with flying colours.

"Well done, son. I knew you could do it," beamed his dad, giving him a manly pat on the back.

His mum hugged him tight. "We're really proud of you, Es."

"Thanks, Mum," he grinned, kissing her head. He felt really proud for the first time in his life.

Soon after, he enrolled on a year-long advanced course at the college.

Even though he was under age, he began drinking in local pubs. He liked the warm atmosphere there. One night, when he and some mates came out of the Barge Aground pub in Barking, a group of older men walked past them and one of them called out, "Hey, nigger!"

"What did you say?" called out Es, turning around.

"I said, 'Hey, nigger'," replied the bloke with a sneer, moving threateningly towards Es.

"Don't call me that," retorted Es, facing him.

The bloke grinned and then caught Es on the chin with a sharp punch, knocking him onto a wall, and then followed it up with a kick in the chest.

Es stood up, clutching his chest, and was about to go for the bloke when his mates grabbed hold of him. "Leave it, Es. Come on, let's go," said one of them.

Walking away, he felt that his pride had been dented.

Occasionally he went to watch West Ham United play away, travelling on the football special trains. Some of the fans would smash up trains and engage in running battles with rival supporters, but Es never got involved. He was careful to keep away from the trouble-makers, thinking that it was pointless.

To increase his fitness, he took up boxing at Dagenham Boxing Club. After a year and a half, Lenny Wilson, one of the trainers, told him that he was a powerful puncher and could make it as an amateur boxer. But he wasn't committed or disciplined enough and used to only go when he felt like it.

One evening, Es was with two mates in Dagenham when one of them said excitedly, "Let's nick a car for a bit of a laugh."

"Can you drive, then?" asked Es, not really sure about nicking a car.

"Yeah, my old man taught me."

His mate began trying the door handles of the cars

parked in a quiet street near Dagenham Heathway station. Eventually, one of the doors clicked open and the three of them clambered in. Next thing, they were speeding away. But at a set of traffic lights they found themselves behind a police car. One of the officers got out and rapped his knuckles on the driver's window.

"How old are you?" he asked.

"Seventeen," lied Paul.

"Can I see your licence?" asked the officer.

Paul went red and admitted he didn't have one.

"I think you three had better come with me to the station," said the officer.

A few weeks later, the three of them appeared at Stratford Magistrate's Court, where each of them was found guilty of taking and driving away without the owner's consent and fined £100. Es felt that he had been stupid to get involved in the escapade. Now, he had to cough up a hundred quid.

He opened a Giro Bank account and eventually saved up enough money to buy a red Yamaha 50 cc moped. The following year, he passed his driving test and bought his first car, a white Morris 1100.

He never went out looking for trouble. In fact, he tried to avoid it. But one night at Oscar's nightclub, at the Green Gate pub in Newbury Park, he got into an argument with a guy at the bar.

"Come on, then. Outside," challenged the guy.

Es didn't want a straightener, but there was no way he was going to back down. "Okay, let's go," he replied with a steely look.

They walked outside and stood facing each other in the car park. Although Es was taller, the other guy was stocky and vicious looking. Es landed the first punch, knocking the guy onto the bonnet of a car. But he hauled himself up immediately and launched a flurry of kicks and punches at Es. Es parried them and drove his fist hard into the guy's face, splitting his lip. The guy lunged at Es with his head and sent him reeling backwards.

Then Es screamed with pain as someone yanked both his arms up his back. "Ah! Leave off!" he shouted.

"You're nicked, nigger," said a voice sharply.

Es wondered what was going on. He was dragged across the car park towards a Ford Transit police van and shoved inside, head first onto the floor, with the foot of someone pressing down on his head and another foot pressing on his right hand.

"What's going on? It was just a straightener," he pleaded, trying to struggle free.

"Yeah?" said a chubby policeman with beady eyes, looking down at him. "Is that right, nigger?"

Another policeman sat on top of him, twisting one of his arms behind his back. It felt like it was coming out of its socket. "Aagh! Let go! Let go!" he cried.

Boots and fists began pummelling him. The beating was savage and it seemed to go on for ages.

Then Es heard a voice order, "That's enough!"

He was then pushed out of the carrier, landing with a thud on the road. Dazed, he began to stand up, clutching his sides. The pain was excruciating. Feeling breathless, he gingerly rubbed his face and then examined the palm of his right hand. It was streaked in blood. Leaning on a wall, he watched as the van pulled away into the traffic.

Chapter Three

On the Doors

Es's next visit to Oscar's had a very different outcome. He was laughing and joking with a group of mates at the bar one Saturday night when he noticed a slim girl with long brown hair standing on her own, waiting to get served. Later on during the evening, he plucked up the courage to ask her for a dance. She told him that her name was Linda, and he discovered that she was five years older than him. That night, he left with her phone number scribbled on the back of his ticket. They met for a drink at a pub in Harold Hill a few days later, and then they started going out together. One evening, when Es met her after work, she said that she had something important to tell him.

"What is it?"

She pursed her lips and then said, "I'm pregnant."

"You what?"

"I'm pregnant. I found out yesterday."

Es didn't know what to say. Pregnant! He'd never given a minute's thought to the fact that Linda might get pregnant. What should he do? He was just nineteen. The idea of becoming a dad had never entered his head.

"Don't worry, Linda. I'll stick by you," he found himself saying, even though he wasn't sure what he meant.

That night, lying awake in bed, he decided that there was only one thing to do: marry her. He didn't know if he loved her, but he liked her. In the morning, he told his dad about his decision.

"Are you sure about this?" his dad asked in a solemn voice.

"I am, Dad."

"Well, you've done the right thing then, son," he replied.

A few months later Es and Linda got married at Langton's registry office in Hornchurch and soon after moved into a second-floor flat in a tower block on the Gascoigne Estate in Barking, an area notorious for drug dealing, violence and vandalism. Es settled into married life and the following year Linda gave birth to Carl.

After training at Dagenham Boxing Club one evening, Es got chatting to a guy he'd known since school.

"So how are things, Es?" he asked, combing his hair in the mirror.

"Okay, mate, but I'm fed up with the job. Painting and decorating isn't going to make me rich."

"Yeah?"

"I need to do something else. I need extra money. I've got a wife and a kid now, you know."

The guy thought for a moment and then said, "Why don't you become a bouncer?"

"A bouncer? What, me?"

"Yeah. You can handle yourself and you're a big strong bloke."

"I'd never thought of bouncing."

"Go down to the Ilford Palais and see if they want anyone. I've heard they're always taking blokes on."

"No, it's not me, mate," Es said, pulling a face. "Too much aggro."

The guy shrugged and slipped on his jacket. "Just a suggestion."

Es dismissed the idea, but then, a few months later, when he was painting a flat in Becontree Heath, he found himself thinking back to that conversation. Then one evening he decided to go to the Palais to see if they had any vacancies. Situated in High Road, Ilford, the Palais was a huge nightclub, and one of the most popular in east London.

"Do you have any vacancies for door staff, mate?" Es asked one of the bouncers standing in the foyer.

"Hang on," he replied gruffly, signalling to a stocky bloke standing near the cloakroom. "You need to speak to the head doorman."

"What's up?" asked the head doorman, coming over.

"I was wondering if you had any jobs going," Es said, trying to appear confident.

"What, for door staff?"

Es nodded, "Yeah."

"Wait a minute," he replied, and then went into the ticket kiosk. He emerged with a sheet of paper and handed it to Es. "Fill this in and then give it back to me."

"Okay," said Es. He leant on a table and began to answer the questions. When he had finished, he handed it back to the head doorman, who glanced at it briefly.

"So you've done a bit of boxing?"

"Yeah."

"Okay, mate, we'll be in touch," the doorman said, slipping the form into his inside pocket.

A couple of weeks later the head doorman phoned. "We'll give you a try and see how you perform," he said. "You're down for Friday and Saturday night. Nine to two. Turn up at about eight-thirty."

"Great," Es replied.

"You'll be on probation for a month. You're a big bloke and you look like you can take care of yourself, but we need to see how you operate in the team. This job's all about teamwork. You have to watch each other's back. Oh, yeah, and you'll need to buy a black suit and a black dickie bow."

"No problem."

"Right, see you at the Palais on Friday. And don't be late. We don't take on bad timekeepers."

"Don't worry. I won't be late. Cheers."

As Friday approached, Es felt a mixture of excitement and nervousness. He was worried that he might do something wrong or not spot trouble. He didn't want to let the other blokes down.

On Friday afternoon, he knocked off early from his painting and decorating job in Tottenham, so that he had enough time to have a bath and make himself look presentable. At eight o'clock, dressed in the new suit he'd bought, he said goodbye to Linda, kissed Carl and set off for the Palais.

Walking through the doors, he felt even more nervous. It suddenly hit him that he'd had no training and he didn't really know what he would be expected to do. The Palais consisted of a large dance floor downstairs, as well as a long bar and a restaurant that served fast food. Upstairs was a horseshoe-shaped balcony and another bar.

There were about a dozen other doormen on duty, along with a woman. Looking at the other members of the team, laughing and joking with each other, he could see how confident and at ease they appeared. He felt he was the outsider. The other blokes weren't particularly friendly, but he could understand this. He was the new boy and he had to prove himself. He knew that they were waiting to see how well he could do the job.

"Es, you float with him," said the head doorman, pointing to a guy with a moustache.

"Float?" said Es.

"Yeah. That means you just float around the club keeping your eyes and ears open. Watch the flash points."

"Flash points?"

"Yeah. Trouble often kicks off around the two bars, in the queue for food and on the dance floor."

Es had been into nightclubs as a punter, of course, but standing on the other side of the line, as a bouncer, was a very different feeling, he soon realised. His first night was pretty uneventful. Apart from helping to eject a few guys who were drunk, and a girl who was abusive to the cloakroom attendant, there was nothing much to deal with. When he left the club, he felt relieved that he'd got his first night out of the way, and that he hadn't made any major mistakes.

The following Saturday night he had to deal with his first bit of serious trouble. Towards the end of the evening, he noticed a guy with a shaved head and a tattoo on his neck arguing with the cloakroom attendant.

"What's the problem?" asked Es, standing a couple of feet away from the guy.

"He doesn't have a ticket. I've told him that I can't give out any jackets without a ticket," said the young girl in the cloakroom.

"That's right, mate. You need a ticket if you want your jacket." The head doorman had spelled out the club rules to Es on the first night.

"I've lost it. And I want my jacket," he said aggressively. Es could tell he was drunk.

"You'll either have to wait until the end of the night or come back tomorrow," said Es calmly.

"No. I want my jacket now!" demanded the guy, stabbing his finger in the air.

"I've told you: no ticket, no jacket. Either wait until the end of the night or come back tomorrow," repeated Es more firmly, hoping the guy would get the message.

The man swore and then tried to head butt him, but he only managed to hit him in the chest. Quickly putting his arm around his neck, Es yanked him backwards across the foyer and bundled him outside and down the steps.

"Now, come back tomorrow if you want your jacket," he said.

"I'm going to come and shoot you," threatened the guy.

Es ignored the threat and just stood there on the steps impassively. The guy then wandered off down the road, swearing and shouting.

"Okay, Es?" asked the head doorman, coming out.

"Yeah, but he said he was going to come back and shoot me."

"Don't worry. You get a lot of that 'I'll be back' stuff. But few of them ever do come back – usually."

During the next few weeks, Es discovered that there was more to being a doorman than acting tough. When he took his turn at the entrance, he had to search punters for weapons. If he found any item that could be used as a weapon, he had to ask the person to collect it at the end of the night. But if he found a six-inch blade on someone, he confiscated it and the person was turned away.

On a busy night, the club could have 1,600 punters coming through the doors. It attracted everyone from villains and second-hand car dealers to solicitors and off-duty coppers. Most of the punters were young, working class and white, and all out for a good time. The thing that Es really noticed at the end of the evening when the music stopped was that people were shouting at each other. They had been doing this all night in order to be heard above the music, and many, partly because of the alcohol, continued speaking at that level.

There was always something to do, such as asking someone not to take their drinks or food from the burger bar onto the dance floor, not to go up to the DJ to ask for requests and not to block the stairs. A common problem was punters leaning over the balcony and tipping their drinks on people below. He also had to check the toilets for people who were taking drugs, having sex, or who had collapsed. He also had to sort out arguments between boyfriends and girlfriends.

Doormen, he soon realised, acted as a magnet to some women because of the power they were seen to possess. It makes some women feel special if they get to know a doorman and they can then brag about this to their mates. There were two girls from West Ham who were known as 'the bouncers' bikes'. It wasn't uncommon for several bouncers to go to a flat with them at the end of the night for sex. But Es never did.

Es gradually got to know the other members of the

team, which included Gary Woods, who, unbeknown to Es, was a member of the National Front; Tony Spittal, a quietly spoken ex-Royal Marine; Dave Golds, a flamboyant guy known as 'Pretty Boy', and who always had lots of women on the go; Roy Andre, who worked on the railways and was a good amateur boxer; Joggsy, a practical joker; Keith Jocelyn, who sold flowers outside Mile End Underground station; Terry Rolfe, who had served in the Royal Navy; Lee White, a volatile, larger than life character and former amateur boxer; Paul Taylor, known as a ducker and diver; Pete Edwards, a former soldier from Leicester; Mars Bar, who always seemed to be looking over his shoulder when he was working; Mad Dog, who had a ferocious temper; Todd, another ex-soldier, who said 'Sweet as a nut' to everything; and Jane, a large, masculine-type lady who came in handy for breaking up fights between women.

Es learned that he had to judge situations very quickly, asking himself whether a punter was drunk, mad or a bit lively. Some people would stand outside shouting threats or kicking the doors. He discovered that there was often a woman behind much of the trouble that broke out.

It didn't take him long to understand how important it was to get the first punch in when trouble broke out. He knew that a moment's hesitation could lead to him ending up on the floor. To be more effective, he began attending a kick-boxing club run by Dave Golds at Sugar House Lane in Stratford. He learned punching and kicking techniques, and showed so much enthusiasm that he cracked a guy's ribs with a kick during one session.

Es became good friends with Terry Rolfe, a 6' 7" man mountain and they did weight training together at Highams gym in Leytonstone. One time at the Palais, Terry was escorting the manageress as she carried the takings from the counter in the foyer to the office upstairs. Es was standing in the foyer with some of the other doormen when a fight broke out with a group of rowdy guys. Terry dropped the cash, ran back downstairs and waded in, putting two of the guys in head locks and heaving them out of the doors. Es put a guy in a Hawaii-style shirt in a bear hug and dragged him outside.

"We'll be back!" yelled the guy in the Hawaii-style shirt. "So you'd better watch out."

Later in the evening, a doorman came up to Es, who was standing at the edge of the dance floor. "Es, that little firm have got back in. They're in the bar."

"Well, how did they do that?"

"Don't know, but we'd better get them out."

Es and three other doormen squeezed their way through the crowded dance floor to the bar.

"Right, you lot. Out!" said Es.

The three guys just laughed.

Es took a step closer. "Are you going, or do we have to make you go?"

"Make us go, then," said the one in the Hawaii-style shirt defiantly.

Es and the other two doormen exchanged glances and then moved in to grab hold of the three guys, who began lashing out at them with their fists. One of them went to pick up his glass off the bar, but Es caught him on the arm with a vicious chop. They managed to shove the guys through the crowd and out into the foyer, where two more doormen joined in. Eventually, the guys were bundled outside and given a few kicks to see them on their way.

Terry then appeared, looking shaken.

"Where were you?" Es said to him, annoyed. "We could have done with you at the bar."

"What do you mean? I was there, mate, and I was stabbed," he said, clutching his thigh.

It was then that Es noticed that Terry's trousers were soaked in blood. "What happened, Terry?"

"One of that little firm pulled out a screwdriver on me," he said with an anguished look.

Terry went off to hospital to have his wound seen to, leaving Es reflecting on how dangerous a job working the doors could be.

* * *

Es's first professional injury happened soon enough. A guy called 'Polly' suddenly broke off a chat with some of the doormen, including Es and Lee, outside the club and quickly disappeared inside. Es was still wondering what was the matter with him when a dozen blokes appeared from nowhere. Where had this lot come from? he wondered. One thing he knew for sure was that they were out for trouble.

"Oi! You! Come here," ordered a bloke wearing a red T-shirt and jeans, pointing at Lee.

"What's the problem, mate?" replied Lee, cautiously walking towards him.

Sensing the worst, Es took a couple of steps behind Lee to watch his back. Before he knew what was happening, the blokes simultaneously whipped out plastic bottles and squirted them in the direction of Lee. Reacting quickly, Lee ducked, and something hit Es in the eye. Instantly, he knew that it was ammonia. The stinging sensation was terrible and he couldn't see anything. Instinctively, he began lashing out wildly with his fists and feet.

Then he felt someone grip his arm and pull him into the club.

"You okay, Es?" asked Pat, the front-of-house manager, slamming the door shut behind him.

"Yeah, but my eye's killing me," he said with a grimace.

"Don't worry. Put some cold water on it."

Later, he discovered that the blokes were really after Polly, who had been seeing the girlfriend of one of them.

Es soon established his reputation by showing that he wasn't frightened to get stuck in when there was trouble in the club. One evening, he was standing on the front steps when several blokes suddenly surrounded him and began raining kicks and punches on him. He fought back, but then felt a crack on his head. One of the guys was clutching a long piece of wood. Before he had time to react, the blokes legged it down the road.

He heard from one of the doormen that the blokes who'd attacked him drank at the Henry Ford pub near the Ford's car factory in Dagenham. It was known as 'the flying bottle' because of the number of fights that took place there. Es decided he would get his revenge.

Later that night, Es and a group of doormen piled into two cars and drove to the Henry Ford – he was raring to go. When they arrived, they found Alan Matthews, known as Fraggle, standing with his doormen at the entrance. He ran the doors at a string of pubs and clubs in London.

"Hello, lads. What can I do for you?" he asked in his typical chirpy manner.

"I'm looking for some blokes who were at the Palais earlier tonight. I've heard they drink here," Es said gruffly, peering over Fraggle's shoulders.

"What do they look like?"

Es described them. "Are they in here?"

"No, not here. Sorry, babes."

But Es didn't believe him. Fraggle was a slippery character, but he was also charismatic and a real charmer. "You sure?"

He shook his head. "Yeah, positive, babes. You won't find them here."

"Hey, Es, there's one of them!" said Lee excitedly, nodding towards some guys sitting at the bar.

Es elbowed his way past Fraggle, followed by his

firm, and pushed through the crowd of drinkers and walked up to a curly haired guy with bulging eyes, who was sitting with a group of mates.

Poking him in the chest, he said, "Remember me?"

"What do you mean?" replied the guy, startled.

Es then slammed his fist into him, sending him reeling back, and then rained a succession of punches down on him. His mates stood back, seeing that Es had a tasty little firm standing behind him. Satisfied that he had done the job, Es turned and walked back out, shooting Fraggle a cold look as he left.

He had now got used to the regular outbreaks of trouble at the Palais and had worked out that within a group of guys on a night out there's always a couple who don't want to fight. A doorman had to be able to pick out the ones he considered the most dangerous and, if necessary, deal with them explosively.

Before he went on the doors he would often go for a drink with Terry to the Havelock in High Road, Ilford, where he became friends with Louis Whittaker and Babyface, who both worked on the doors at the Penthouse, a nightclub at the other end of High Road. A stocky, strong black guy with shortish Afro hair and a thin moustache, Louis was a sports fanatic who was always dressed in a tracksuit. Es used to find it amusing when he suddenly broke into West Indian patois during a conversation. Babyface, a bulky, fresh-faced guy who was a lethal kick boxer, was more reserved.

By now, Es was working four nights a week on the doors. He loved it, even though he was only earning twelve quid a shift. In fact, he'd have done it for nothing. He felt he was good at it and that he was accepted and appreciated. For the first time he really felt he fitted in somewhere.

He was also still working as a painter and decorator. In order to earn extra money, he bought a rusty second-hand white Volkswagen van and started up a mobile valeting service.

It was rare for him to get out of the club before 2.30 am. Afterwards, he would often go with some of the other doormen to nearby Sal's Restaurant, which stayed open throughout the night, for a drink and something to eat. Sal was a friendly bloke with a Mediterranean complexion. He liked having a group of doormen in his restaurant, as he knew that if he had any trouble he could call on them.

*   *   *

One evening at the Palais, Es was taking a break in the restroom which led off the balcony when one of the doormen said, "Have a draw on this."

"What is it?"

"A spliff. Go on – have a go."

"Yeah, okay," Es said, taking the spliff from him. He'd never taken drugs before.

"What do you reckon?"

Es drew deeply on it. "Yeah. It's good."

He got up, swaying slightly, and left the restroom. He thought a group of doormen standing on the opposite side of the balcony were laughing at him. He stormed through the crowds of punters and bellowed at the top of his voice, "What are you lot looking at?"

The doormen stared at him, wondering what the matter was.

His head spinning, he then made his way downstairs to the foyer, where Terry and several other doormen were.

"Es, come in here," said Terry, motioning to a small room.

Es followed him in.

"Calm down, Es," said Terry. "What's up?"

"I don't know," muttered Es, looking frantically around him.

Seeing that he wasn't getting much sense out of Es, Terry left the room and then Todd came in.

"What's up, mate?" asked Todd cheerily.

"I'm all right. Leave me alone."

"Yeah. Sweet as a nut."

As soon as he said this, Es aimed a punch at him, but it missed and smashed the glass covering the electricity box on the wall. Terry then rushed back in, put his arm around him and led him outside to get some fresh air.

"You'll be okay, Es," said Terry as they walked towards the flyover.

"My head's going round," murmured Es.

"That's because it's the first time you've taken dope."

"Well, I ain't taking it again, that's for sure."

Leslie Grantham, who plays Dirty Den in *EastEnders*, had been booked to visit the club and sign autographs. Terry and Es were asked to shadow the actor. Amidst all the people clamouring around him, Es was over the moon, feeling that he had taken a first step towards a childhood dream of being a bodyguard.

Tensions among the doormen could rise very easily. One night, Lee White got into an argument on the steps of the club with a scruffy bloke in a denim jacket. Lee told him he couldn't come in because he was wearing trainers. The bloke began swearing and then stormed off, shouting that he was coming back to do Lee.

"I'm going to have him," snarled Lee.

"What do you mean?" replied Es, wondering why he was so angry. This sort of incident was quite common at the Palais.

"I'm going after him," Lee said, running to his car, which was parked at the side of the Palais. He jumped in and roared off down the High Road after the unsuspecting bloke. Es set off down the road after him. He watched helplessly as Lee drove the car at the bloke, who just managed to avoid being hit by diving into a shop doorway. Startled passers-by stood back as Lee leapt out of the car, screaming and waving a knife in the air. The bloke sprinted across the road and up a staircase that led to a small shopping precinct.

"Lee! Lee! Stop!" shouted Es, chasing after him. Es

bounded up the staircase, his heart pounding, and caught up with him at the top. "Lee, leave it! It's not worth it."

Lee stopped and turned around. He seemed unsure of what to do. Eventually, he said, "Yeah, you're right."

"Forget him, mate."

When the management heard about the incident, Lee was sacked on the spot. Feeling that he'd been unfairly treated, Es resigned in support. Someone suggested Es went to work for Fraggle. He didn't much care for Fraggle, especially after the incident at the Henry Ford, but he needed some work. A phone call to Fraggle produced an immediate job offer on the doors at a pub across the river in Blackheath.

Es was part of a team of eight. They were all bored stiff as the pub was dead. Why did they need so many bouncers, and during the day as well as the evening? he wondered, looking around at the empty tables.

"It's a bit quiet here tonight," he said to one of the barmaids.

"What do you expect?" she replied.

"What do you mean?" he asked, puzzled.

"You must have heard about the bloke who was shot here last night."

"Shot! No, I didn't know." Es was annoyed that he hadn't been told about this.

The next three nights at the pub were as quiet as the first one. Then Es was sent to a busy pub in Norwood as part of a team of over a dozen bouncers. On one of the nights when he wasn't working, several van loads of the Chelsea Head Hunters, a notorious group of football hooligans, turned up and caned all the doormen. He worked for a few weeks at Roxanne's in Stratford before being offered his job back at the Palais. But when he returned, he got the impression that the management saw him as a rebel.

With painting and decorating, his car valet jobs and working the doors, he was spending little time at home with Linda and Carl. This troubled him, but he felt that he was now someone and that he had an identity.

He'd been at the Palais for about eighteen months when, one night while sitting in the restroom, he found himself saying to Terry, "I'm going to start my own door firm."

"You what?" said Terry, looking incredulous.

"Yeah, my own company," he repeated, feeling a bit awkward. "Why not?"

"Well, good luck to you," said Joggsy, casually looking up from *The Sun*. He clearly thought Es was dreaming.

"Yeah, good luck," said Terry.

Es didn't know why he'd said this. The idea of him running his own door company seemed a bit unreal. But, at the same time, a part of him felt that he could do it.

Es at 16 years old with his first independent form of transport, a Yamaha moped.

Es sharing a drink and chat with a regular customer at The Penthouse nightclub in Ilford.

Chapter Four

The Firm

In early 1984, Es left the Palais and went to work with Louis and Babyface at the Penthouse, a night-club on the top of Harrison Gibson's department store at the other end of High Road, Ilford. Like the Palais, it was a busy place, though smaller. It had formerly been called the Room at the Top but, after regular outbreaks of trouble, it was closed and reopened under a new name. The crowd who went there tended to be older than those who went to the Palais.

It wasn't long before Es had to deal with trouble. At the end of a Saturday night, Micky Foster, an amateur boxer, was standing with some mates in the foyer near the lift, looking unhappy.

"What's the matter, Micky?" he asked, wandering up to him.

"Nah, nothing, Es," he shrugged.

"Come on, mate. Something's up. Tell me what it is."

"There's a big group of blokes over there and they've

been winding me and my mates up. They just want a tear-up. It's nothing. I'll let it go."

Es knew the guys he meant. They were a rowdy lot who were celebrating the release of one of their mates from prison. Micky was worried that they might be waiting for him outside the club, but he wouldn't admit it. "Listen, Micky, I'll get some of the guys and we'll come down with you," said Es.

So Es, Louis and John the Kickboxer, the head doorman and a former champion kick boxer, went down in the lift with Micky and his mates. And sure enough the group of blokes were hanging around on the opposite side of the road, looking set for a ruck. Es noticed a police car parked outside a take-away. He was relieved. These blokes probably wouldn't try anything. But then the panda put the blues and twos on and sped off.

John went over to the group in an attempt to try and prevent a fight breaking out. But Es could see from the body language that the group were not listening. Es, Louis, Micky and his mates wandered across the road and stood behind John. A stocky bloke started swearing at them and then grabbed the shoulder of one of Micky's mates.

"What do you think you're doing? Get your hands off him," retorted Es, moving towards him.

"What? Do you want some as well?" threatened the guy.

"I don't mind if I do," said Es, taking up a boxing stance, feigning a punch and then driving his fist into the guy's jaw, sending him staggering backwards. That was the signal for it to kick off. The two groups went at each other in a flurry of punches and kicks. Es caught one guy with a right hook and another with a flying kick. Out of the corner of his eye, he saw Louis mercilessly pounding a bloke with ginger hair. There was the sound of bottles being smashed somewhere.

Then Es heard a police siren in the distance. He saw that Micky was kneeling over a guy and furiously smashing his head on the pavement.

"Micky! Leave it!" he shouted.

The Old Bill appeared from several directions and waded into the middle of the fight. They grabbed the guy Es had hit. He struggled to get free, shouting at Es that he was going to shoot him. Eventually he was bundled into the back of a police van.

"What's been going on here, then?" asked a stern copper.

"Usual idiots trying to cause trouble, officer," replied Es matter-of-factly.

The copper nodded knowingly. "Okay. We'll be on our way."

Es had now learned to expect the unexpected when working on the doors. One night at the Penthouse, he was patrolling the dance floor when an angry-looking blonde woman came up to him.

"'Ere, there's a guy over there who tried to touch me up," she said.

"Can you point him out?"

"Yeah. It's 'im," she said, jabbing her finger in the

direction of the far corner. "The one in the white T-shirt and jeans."

He realised she was talking about Ron, the brother-in-law of Snoopy, the club DJ. Es and Snoopy had first met at the Havelock and had become good mates. Es asked one of the other doormen to have a quiet word with Snoopy and ask him to keep his brother-in-law under control. But at the end of the night Es discovered that Ron had made a lewd suggestion to the woman running the cloakroom.

After the club had closed, Es was sitting at a table by the archway near the bar, having a drink with Ray and Mal, the joint managers, and some other doormen. Ron was at the far end talking loudly to Snoopy as he put his records away. 'That's it. I've had enough of him,' Es said to himself and leapt up from the table and stormed towards Ron.

"You might be Snoopy's brother-in-law, but you should show some respect when you're here," he shouted, standing in front of him.

Ron laughed. "Leave it out. What's up with you?"

Leaning back, he lined himself up and slammed his fist hard into Ron's face. Ron let out a gasp and crashed to the floor and a couple of his teeth went flying. Es coolly turned around and walked towards the lift.

"Es, that was out of order," called out Ray sternly, shaking his head. "There was no need for it."

"What he said was out of order," growled Es. "I'm off home."

A couple of days later, the Old Bill turned up at Es's house and arrested him. He was taken to Ilford nick and charged with grievous bodily harm. He heard on the grapevine that Snoopy was going to give evidence against him in court. If he did, this would strengthen Ron's case and he might get sent down. He needed to do something. Thinking it was wiser not to visit Snoopy, he arranged to meet Joe Green, a doorman, at the entrance to Plaistow underground station. Joe was a mate of Snoopy's.

"Snoopy says that he has to give evidence because Ron is his brother-in-law," said Green.

"Well, at the end of the day, tell him, me and him have been like family," said Es.

Green nodded.

"Tell him that if he's going to grass me up, he'd better get running," continued Es.

"Okay, I'll tell him," said Joe. "That it?"

"Yeah, that's all."

Soon after, Es appeared at the magistrate's court and pleaded not guilty. A few months later, he was standing in the dock at Snaresbrook Crown Court. The charge had been changed to actual bodily harm. He admitted hitting Ron, but pleaded self-defence. When Snoopy entered the witness box, he told the court that Es had attacked Ron for no reason. The jury found Es guilty.

"Mr Kaitell," began the judge, "on this occasion I am not going to give you a custodial sentence. Instead, I am going to fine you five hundred pounds. You will also pay four hundred pounds to cover the dental costs incurred by your actions against the victim, as well as the court costs. Have you anything to say?"

"No, your honour," murmured Es, feeling relief – but also resentment at having to pay for Ron's teeth. Shortly after, he heard that Snoopy had gone to live in Spain.

The following week at the Penthouse, Es noticed a group of blokes in the corner. One of them, a slim guy in a smart blue suit, kept staring at him. He'd better be on his guard, he thought to himself. This bloke looked as if he might be out for a tear-up.

A little later on, he was standing by the archway with Louis and Babyface when he spotted the bloke making his way across the dance floor towards them.

The bloke stood in front of them. "Okay?"

"Yeah. And you?" replied Es, wondering what the guy was up to.

The bloke nodded and then said in a Geordie accent, "I work for Norstead Leisure. We're building a leisure complex at Fairlop Waters, near Barkingside. We're going to have a nightclub, bar, restaurant, golf course, indoor children's adventure centre and sailing."

"Sounds good," said Louis.

"We'll be needing some security when it opens. Would you be interested?"

"Might be," said Babyface.

"I've been watching you and I like the way you work."

"Cheers," said Es, feeling flattered.

Es felt a tinge of excitement as he drove along the A123 towards Fairlop Waters a few months later for the opening night of the bar, called Dalton's. As it was a Monday night, it had been decided that just Es and Louis would work the door. Babyface would join them at the weekend when it would be busier. This was a new chapter beginning, he told himself as he parked the car and then made his way across the car park towards the two-storey building, which was situated in between a large lake and a golf course. Dalton's was downstairs, along with a restaurant, while upstairs was Crews nightclub.

"Many in?" Es asked Louis, who was standing at the entrance.

"A few," replied Louis. "But I bet it'll be packed later on."

" We've got a problem," interrupted the manageress anxiously.

"What's up?" Es asked, not really expecting trouble so early on in the evening.

"There's a group of guys in the bar who are being abusive to the staff and helping themselves to drinks."

"Okay, I'll go and take a look," said Es.

Wandering inside, he scanned the bar for the trouble-makers. He recognised them instantly. One of them was built like a giant freezer, one was small and stocky, and the other skinny. They were a loud, aggressive bunch. He returned to Louis on the door.

"Might have a problem with this lot," he said.

"How many are there?" asked Louis.

"Three of them. I don't think theyre going to go quietly."

Ten minutes later, another member of staff came out and told him that the guys were causing trouble again. Es returned to the bar, where the guys were laughing and knocking back pints of lager one after the other. Louis followed at a discreet distance.

"Excuse me," Es said, standing alongside the freezer. "Do you mind if I have a word?"

The freezer spun round. "What do you want?"

"The bar staff are here to work and serve you, not to be abused," continued Es in a calm voice.

"Yeah?"

"Yeah. And don't help yourself to drinks."

"We're only having a laugh, mate," grinned the stocky one, lighting a cigarette and blowing a circle of smoke into the air.

"Yeah, just here for a good night, pal," said the freezer, reaching for his pint.

Es remained impassive. "I'm asking you nicely. If there's any more of it, you're out."

Es and Louis then returned to the entrance, unconvinced that the guys would heed the warning. Ten minutes later, another member of staff came out and said that the guys were causing trouble again. Es and Louis swiftly went back to the bar.

"I'm sorry, but I'm going to have to ask you to leave," said Es firmly to the three guys.

"What, do you fancy yourself then? Do you want

it?" sneered the freezer, stepping towards him.

"Come on then. Outside," snapped back Es. He wanted to resolve the problem peacefully, as it was the first night, but he could see that this wasn't going to happen.

"No, Es," said Louis, placing his hand on Es's arm.

Ignoring him, he made his way towards the entrance, with the freezer following him.

On leaving the building, Es walked towards the area between the club and the golf course, in order not to be in full view of any punters in the car park. Listening to the freezer's footsteps behind him, he suddenly stopped, turned round and drove a ferocious punch into his face, sending him staggering backwards. He swayed one way and then the other and then slumped to the floor.

Panting heavily, Es stood looking down at him. Blood was dribbling out of the corner of his mouth. 'That will teach you,' he thought to himself, putting his tie back on. But then his satisfaction turned to panic when he realised that the bloke wasn't moving. There wasn't a twitch from him.

He hurried back to the entrance. "Lou! I think I've killed him! What am I going to do?"

"You what?"

"He's lying outside and he's not moving. I've killed him, Lou!"

"Calm down, Es," said Louis. "Hold on. You don't know he's dead."

Es was worried. He went into the bar, trying to

think what to do. Was he dead? If he was, he'd be done for murder. Should he make a run for it? What should he do? His life passed before him.

Returning to the entrance, relief swept through him when he saw the guy being propped up against the wooden fence by his mates. He was moving.

"Thank God for that, Lou!"

"Told you not to panic," replied Louis. "Hang on, though, he's coming back."

The freezer was walking unsteadily back towards the building, with his mates alongside him.

"Here we go again," said Es to Louis as the freezer stopped a couple of feet away from him.

Then, to Es's amazement, he extended his hand. Es thought for a moment and then warily shook it, half-expecting the bloke to try and land a punch. Instead, he turned around and walked towards the car park.

"You don't know who we are!" screamed one of his mates. "We'll burn the place down."

"We're going to have you!" shouted another one. "We'll be back."

Es stood watching them as they walked off down the lane towards the main road. He was unconcerned about their threats. He'd heard plenty of threats since he began working on the doors. All he could feel was relief that the bloke was still alive.

As Fairlop Waters needed the doors covering seven nights a week, Es, Louis and Babyface decided that they would hire some extra staff. When Babyface left Fairlop Waters, Es and Louis decided to form a company. They called it WK Security after their surnames, Whittaker and Kaitell. They had headed paper, business cards and flyers printed.

Es and Louis began recruiting a number of guys who they knew could handle themselves and they also devised a call-out service. In other words, if there was too much trouble for the door staff to handle in a particular venue, one of them would phone Es or Louis, who would call up extra door staff to help out. As the reputation of WK spread, they started getting what they called dirty jobs – pubs no one else would touch because there was too much trouble.

One day, the area manager of a brewery phoned Es about running the doors at the Cherry Tree in Dagenham. "We've been having a lot of trouble at the pub. The security company we have are useless. One night, they even sent a crippled bloke to work on the doors. Could you do a better job?" he asked.

"Definitely, mate," replied Es confidently. "Let me come over and have a chat with you and then we can talk about what you need."

Pleased with how well WK handled the Cherry Tree, the area manager asked them to run the doors at several other pubs, including one on the South Circular road, which they had temporarily closed down because a notorious local family was causing trouble and had firebombed it. Es and five doormen stayed there for a week in order to protect the stock and send a warning signal to the family.

They were also asked to run the doors at Top Touch

nightclub in Dagenham. The two Asian brothers who owned it had been getting hassled by some local yobs who apparently didn't like Asians being in what was a predominantly white area. Within a week the hassle had stopped. After coming up against Es and his team, the yobs wisely decided to go elsewhere for a night out.

The brothers then gave Es some 'debt-collecting' jobs. Apart from the nightclub, they had other business interests. The money was good and, usually, Es didn't have to resort to force to get someone to pay up.

Around this time, WK were also asked to provide security for boxing promoter Alan Mortlock at a major international kick-boxing show at the Picket's Lock Centre in Edmonton, north London. Given the kind of characters who turn up at boxing shows, there's always the potential for trouble. The evening, however, passed without any major incidents.

It wasn't long before some of the most feared faces in the East End signed up for work with WK. They included Peter Defreitas, the former manager of Nigel Benn; Billy Gow, classified by the Old Bill as one of Britain's most dangerous criminals; Vic Dark, who had been in prison for armed robbery; Steve Hunt, a member of a well-known East End family; Carlton Leach and Matthew Thomas, who had both been leading members of West Ham United's feared Inter City Firm (ICF). Also working for Es was Scouse Pete, who, some years later, was to be the cause of a chain of events that would turn Es's life upside down.

* * *

One night, Es, Louis and a few other doormen went up to the West End. After visiting a few pubs, they went to a Greek restaurant in Soho for a meal.

"You know what?" said Es, knocking back another dark rum.

"What?" said Louis.

"We're like a family."

"Yeah, I suppose we are," Louis replied.

"We are," grinned Es. "I mean, we always watch each other's back and help each other out."

"Let's drink to us," said Louis, picking up his glass and standing up.

They all raised their glasses and cheered, "To the family."

Family . . . Es had felt that his marriage to Linda had been crumbling apart for some time. Linda and he were not getting on. They now had a daughter, Natalie, as well as Carl. All that had prevented him from leaving was the children. He didn't want to be apart from them.

One night at Fairlop Waters he met a woman called Carron and they began a relationship. Soon after, he left Linda and moved into Carron's upstairs flat in Empress Avenue, Ilford. He welcomed a new start with someone else, but he was overcome with guilt about the end of the marriage and leaving Carl and Natalie.

He turned the loft of Carron's flat into an office. Running his own company gave him a buzz. He put on a suit when he met clients and he soon learned the lesson in business that most people always want to get more and pay less. Pubs often only want to put one bouncer on a door to keep their costs down, but WK would never put just one bouncer on a door. They turned down so much work because they wouldn't do one-man doors. If there was a serious outbreak of trouble at a pub, Es could have a mini-army ready for action in minutes. This enhanced the reputation of WK.

It was stressful running a security company, so both Es and Louis welcomed the opportunity to occasionally spend a weekend at Redworth Hall Hotel, an Elizabethan manor house set in twenty-five acres of woodland near Newton Aycliffe in County Durham. Run by Norstead Leisure, who owned the Fairlop Waters leisure complex, it had a swimming pool, sauna and classy restaurant.

In August 1988 Es received a phone call one morning to say that his dad had died of a heart attack. The news numbed him, even though he knew that his dad hadn't been well for some time. Watching the coffin being lowered into the grave at Upney Cemetery, he fought back the tears. His adopted parents had been married for fifty-seven years. He placed his arm around his adopted mum and said softly, "He was a good man and a good dad to me. I'm going to miss him."

Sobbing, his mum looked up at him. "He loved you very much, Es. And he was very proud of you."

Es and Louis were called into the general manager's office one evening at Fairlop Waters.

"Listen, you've got to get rid of Billy."

"What do you mean?" Es said with surprise. "He's one of our best doormen."

"I've just had the police on the phone. They said if we don't get rid of him, we'll lose the licence for Crews. They reckon he's one of the most dangerous men in the country."

"Billy's got a reputation, yeah, but he's the perfect gentleman. I've never even seen him throw a punch," said Es.

"It's true. Billy's a top doorman," added Louis.

"That may be so, but I can't afford to have the licence for Crews put at risk. He'll have to go."

Es didn't relish having to tell such a good doorman that he was no longer required, but in the circumstances he had no option. Es went up to Billy at the entrance. "Billy, can I have a word?"

"Sure, Es. What's up?"

"Billy, we're mates, you know that, and you're doing a blinding job on the doors. But we've been told we've got to get rid of you. If we don't, the Old Bill will shut the club down."

"Why? I've not caused any problems."

"I know, mate," said Es. "I don't want to let you go, but it's not my decision."

Billy nodded resignedly. "Yeah, I can see that. No

problem. I understand."

Es was very unhappy at having to let Billy go.

* * *

One night, Es was standing in the lobby of Crews, explaining to a woman how to book a cab, when he heard shouting from the club upstairs. He bounded up the stairs to see what the commotion was.

"Paul's stabbed someone!" said one of the door staff, coming out of the club. Paul was a doorman who was off duty that night.

"You what?"

"Yeah. He's done a geezer with that coach party."

Entering the club, Es was confronted by an angry crowd, screaming and shouting.

"Where is he?" demanded a hatchet-faced woman with a tattoo on her arm.

"I don't know," said Es, figuring that Paul had probably legged it down the fire escape at the back.

"If you don't tell us where he is, we're going to tell the Old Bill it was you," threatened another woman.

"Look, I don't know where he is. I've told you."

As he said this, several coppers appeared.

"It's him," said the woman, pointing at Es. "He did it."

"Right, you're coming with us," said a copper, grabbing Es by the arm.

Es said nothing as he was led away to a waiting police van and taken to Barkingside nick and put in a cell. A short while later, he was sitting in an interview room with two detectives.

"Right, Mr Kaitell. So what have you got to say?" said the first detective.

"I'm saying nothing," replied Es.

"Well, we have a witness to say that you stabbed a man," said the second one.

"I'm saying nothing until I see my brief."

"So, if you didn't do it, who did?" asked the first one.

"No comment." There was no way Es was going to be a grass.

"Listen," said the second one, leaning across the table, "you're wasting your time and our time, so you might as well get it over with. Who did it?"

"No comment."

Seeing that Es was resolute, the detectives, frustrated, abandoned the interview and he was taken back to the cell to wait for Brian Groves, a solicitor – known as the Flying Brief because he rode a motorbike – who visited clients in police custody. As he was an ex-copper, he was disliked by the Old Bill. When he arrived, Es explained what had happened at the club.

"Don't worry. They won't be able to make this stick," said Brian in his thick West Country accent.

"You reckon."

He took off his glasses, blew on them and wiped them with his handkerchief. "Definitely. Don't worry."

However, Es was later charged with grievous bodily harm with intent and released. He felt he was being fitted up. All the Old Bill had to go on was an allegation made by one woman. What's more, he knew that they had been given a description of Paul by a punter at the club. He and Paul looked nothing like each other. Paul was of Mediterranean complexion and shorter than Es. But he reckoned that the Old Bill would like to nail him because of the people he mixed with.

A few weeks later, he appeared at Barkingside Magistrate's Court, where he was committed for trial at Snaresbrook Crown Court. He was worried. With no real evidence, he had thought that the charge would be dropped, but now a prison sentence was becoming a possibility, even though he was innocent.

He went to his solicitor's office in Walthamstow.

"I'm worried," said Es. "How has it gone this far. I didn't touch the bloke. I was downstairs."

"Well, they don't have a case, so don't be," said the solicitor, leaning back in his chair and twirling his pen round.

"Yeah, but what am I looking at if they find me guilty?"

"Probably a seven."

"Seven!"

"But they won't find you guilty."

Es wasn't reassured by his words. He didn't have a lot of faith in either the justice system or the Old Bill. His anxiety increased as the day of the court case neared. On the morning of the trial, he felt a gloom descend on him as he drove to Snaresbrook Crown Court. By the end of the week he could well be banged up in a cell in Pentonville or somewhere. He sat through the trial, listening to various witnesses and the arguments of the prosecution barrister and his defence. Looking at the jury, his spirits began to lift a little. Surely they would be able to see that the case against him didn't stand up.

After lunch on the final day of the trial, he returned to the dock, feeling anxious. The judge took his seat and then suddenly announced, "Take him down."

Es felt the prison officer's hand on his arm. Startled, he looked in panic across at his barrister. His barrister leapt up from his seat and said, "Excuse me, your honour, we haven't had the verdict. The jury haven't come back in yet."

"Ah. Quite right," said the judge, clearly embarrassed. Turning to the clerk of court, he said, "Please ask the jury to return."

The jury filed in and took their seats.

"How do you find the defendant? Guilty or not guilty?" asked the judge.

The foreman replied, "Not guilty, your honour."

Es breathed a deep sigh and shook his head.

* * *

Not long after this, the general manager of Crews called Es and Louis into his office.

"Crews is going to close," he said.

"Why?"

"The police have told me that there's too much

trouble happening here."

"But there's hardly ever any trouble," said Es.

"What about the stabbing?"

"But that was a one-off," said Louis.

The general manager shook his head. "I'm sorry, but the club's going to be closed."

To drown their sorrows, Es and Louis met up with a couple of mates in Ilford for a drink. As they were walking along the High Road, singing, a police van pulled up alongside them. A copper with a large nose stuck his head out of the window. "You lot, shut it!" he barked.

"What do you mean?" asked Es, annoyed. "What's your problem?"

"Don't be lippy."

"We're not doing anything wrong."

"Keep it quiet or we'll nick you."

"We're having a sing-song, that's all. What are you picking on us for?" Es wondered if the fact that they were all black had anything to do with being stopped.

Then police cars and vans suddenly appeared from everywhere and a crowd of coppers surrounded the four of them.

"Now, shut your mouth. This is your last chance," said the copper in the van.

"Yeah, otherwise you'll all be nicked," added a younger copper.

"Take off your blue suit, throw away your warrant card and I'll slap you all over the place," retorted Es.

Unbeknown to Es, a large group of black people

standing outside the Palais were watching intently. This seemed to make the Old Bill uneasy.

"Right, on your way, you lot," said a sergeant, glancing across the road.

*   *   *

Ever since school Es had hated bullies, so when he heard that some blokes had attacked a young chef who worked in the restaurant at Fairlop Waters with CS gas, he was fuming. The chef was just a kid. After making some enquiries, he discovered that the attackers frequented Epping Forest Country Club.

One night Es, Matthew Thomas and some mates went there in search of them. They found them sitting at a table in the bar.

"Can I have a chat with you outside?" said Es in a voice that showed that he was giving an order rather than asking a question.

"No, you can't," replied a guy in a bomber jacket.

"Okay, we'll chat here," replied Es, pulling a chair up to the table. "What are you doing bullying a seventeen-year-old kid?"

"What you on about?"

"You know what I'm talking about."

"Got the wrong blokes, mate," said a guy with a pony-tail. The other two blokes looked worried and said nothing.

"I don't think so," said Es, lowering his voice and leaning across the table.

"Listen, mate. I'm telling you that you have. Now get lost," said the guy with the pony-tail, blowing cigarette smoke towards Es.

As soon as he said this, Es exploded. Leaping up, he drove his fist into the jaw of the guy with the pony-tail and then punched the one wearing the bomber jacket in the stomach. Both of them collapsed onto the floor, sending the glasses on the table flying. Customers sitting nearby scattered.

"Want some more?" asked Es, his fists clenched.

The two guys looked up and shook their heads.

"Well, that'll teach you not to be bullies."

The next day, Es heard that the management at the Epping Forest Country Club was unhappy with what had happened. Realising that he had taken liberties with the doormen on duty, the following evening, he drove to the club and left a large bottle of pink champagne for the doormen. He knew that if an incident like that had happened when he was running the door, he would have been furious.

Es with his youngest son Aaron, just weeks after
being left for dead at the Ilford Palais.

Working the doors at a pub.

Chapter Five

Gangland

"Things are going well, mate," said Es, signalling to the barmaid for another Golden Terror and slapping a tenner down on the bar.

Louis grinned, tapping his feet to the pounding music. "Yeah, man, we're doing okay. We're doing good."

It was a cold, drizzly Thursday night in January 1990, and Es and Louis were at Stopouts wine bar and nightclub in Ilford, which was run by Andy Pohl, a blond-haired former Royal Marine commando. Es and Louis usually went to Stopouts on Thursdays and ended up drinking in the bar at the back with a crowd of people they knew. Es, Louis, Tutu, a big tall guy with a wide smile, and Bill, a Ugandan guy who drove mini-cabs, were known as 'the sliders', because when they danced, they slid across the floor, moving their heads and feet in unison.

WK now supplied door staff to eighteen pubs and clubs, including the bar at Fairlop Waters (the Old Bill had closed down the nightclub), the White Hart in Brentwood, the Cherry Tree in Dagenham, Reflections in Stratford, the Havelock in Ilford, and Antics in Bow. They had also supplied security for events such as raves in disused factories; kick-boxing shows; charity nights at top West End hotels, where stars from TV shows such as EastEnders and The Bill auctioned personal items; and American classic car rallies in North Weald, Essex. All the money Es and Louis made from supplying door staff to Stopouts went straight back into the club's till. But they weren't bothered. They just wanted a good time. Although dark rum was Es's favourite drink, on Thursdays he'd always drink Golden Terror, which was made up of gin, tequila, vodka, Southern Comfort and orange juice, in a half-pint glass.

"Hey, Lou," said Es, ordering another Golden Terror.

"What, mate?"

"See those two geezers in the corner?"

Louis turned around. "Yeah?"

"They've been laughing at me."

"Yeah?"

"Yeah. And I'm going to have a word."

Es pushed his way through the crowded bar to where the two guys were sitting. "What you looking at?" he roared.

"Nothing, mate," said one of them feebly.

"You've been staring at me, haven't you?"

"No, mate. Honestly."

Es snapped and smashed the guy in the face with his fist. Then he grabbed the other one by the neck, pulled his fist back and caught him with a right hook. Shocked, they both cowered there, clutching their faces and groaning. Unaware that other customers were staring at him, Es then turned around and went nonchalantly back to the bar and ordered another drink.

Around this time, he was invited to become the assistant manager of the Havelock pub. Now that he had packed up painting and decorating and his car valet work, he figured that it would not only provide extra income but it would also be useful experience. The manager, Paul Armer, trained him on the job. After six months, he was offered the chance to manage Stopouts, as Andy Pohl had been sacked. But Es didn't want to take on the job if it would offend Andy, whom he'd had a good working relationship with.

"No mate, it won't bother me," said Andy when Es told him about the job offer.

Es thought for a moment. "Listen, I've had an idea. You're out of a job now, so why don't you be my operations manager?" Es knew that Louis would like Andy on the team.

"Yeah?"

"Yeah. It would be right up your street. You'd be in charge of drawing up the rotas for the door staff, assessing venues, dealing with any complaints and organising call-outs. I'll give you a pager so you can be contacted."

Es was delighted when Andy agreed to take the job, as he was a very well-organised guy and someone who would handle the staff well. And he would also be calm in a crisis.

Without realising it, he was becoming more and more aggressive. One night, he and Carron were coming out of Stopouts when a guy with long hair made a rude remark about her as he got into his Ford Escort.

"Oi! Don't you talk to my missus like that," yelled Es angrily.

The bloke turned around and looked at him, shrugged and then drove off.

"Carron, get in the car. I'm not going to let him get away with that."

Es accelerated away and set off after the bloke down High Road, Ilford. The traffic was heavy and he had a job keeping sight of him. Seeing the Escort swing right into Connaught Lane, he overtook a bus and sped after him. The bloke had stopped halfway down the road. Es screeched to a halt behind him, leapt out of the car and smashed his fist through the window. The bloke wasn't there.

He scanned up and down the dark street, but there was no sign of him. Then, looking down at his right hand, he saw that it was covered in blood and that his thumb was partly severed. "Damn!" he said. His right hand was his main weapon. After waiting several hours in the accident and emergency unit at King George's Hospital, he eventually got to see a doctor, who sewed his thumb back. When the doctor asked him what he did for a living and he replied that he was a doorman, he warned, "Well, make sure you don't hit anyone with this hand. If you do, you might have problems."

A few days later, John the Kickboxer phoned. Es could tell from the tone of his voice that something was up.

"What's up, John, mate?"

"Robert was beaten up by the bouncers at that club in Ealing he was working at. They took a real liberty with him. Would you come along and bring the firm?"

Es wasn't surprised at this news. Robert was a loud, arrogant bloke who was always getting himself into tear-ups.

"Yeah, no problem," said Es. "I'll get the boys together." Es agreed to do this out of a sort of loyalty to John, whom he felt a sense of gratitude towards for taking him on at the Penthouse.

After putting the phone down, he went up to the loft, sat down at his desk and opened his black contact book. He scanned the names and began to draw up a list of guys who would be up for going over to west London. He then phoned each one of them, explained what had happened and then asked them to meet him in Ealing early on Wednesday evening – and come tooled up. Es knew that there wouldn't be many punters in the club at that time of the evening. He managed to get a team of about fifteen guys together, including Matthew Thomas, Shane and Dave Golds.

A barmaid Robert knew at the club had given him

information about the bouncers working there. It turned out that they weren't linked to any major faces, as far as he knew. 'Always good news,' thought Es, when he heard this.

The following Wednesday evening, Es, John and three of his firm drove across London to Ealing, tooled up with coshes, ammonia and knuckle-dusters. Es carried a cosh in the inside pocket of his long leather jacket. As they sped along the Westway flyover, he spotted St Mary's Hospital next to Paddington station, where he had been born, and he found himself reflecting on his life. He was thirty-two, divorced and had two children, and he made his living from sorting out trouble. How different his life had turned out from that of his dad.

After getting caught up in a traffic jam at Hanger Lane for what seemed like ages, they eventually reached Ealing and parked in a side street off Uxbridge Road and then made their way to a pub near the club to meet the rest of the firm. After all the guys arrived in the pub, John and Es left and set off for the club. The plan was for John and Es to go in first and then the others to follow, at intervals, in pairs or groups of three, so that the bouncers wouldn't suspect anything. Once inside, they would meet at one of the bars and then check how many doormen there were and where they were plotted.

"Evening," said one of the doormen.

"Evening, mate," replied Es, casually walking past him and into the foyer.

He heard the sound of the doors being bolted behind him. Startled, he spun around, only to find himself surrounded by a dozen doormen. Es and John looked at each other and then at the doormen.

"What's up, guys?" asked John, blinking.

"You're coming with us," said a bouncer with slicked-back hair, pointing towards a set of doors.

This looked like a big problem. What should they do? Make a run for it? Front it out? Before he had time to decide, he was being marched across the dance floor, through another set of doors, and then down a corridor towards an office. As one of the bouncers opened the door, Es heard what sounded like several gun shots coming from outside. What was going on? Shooting was the last thing he'd expected to hear.

Inside the smoky office was a mean-looking Asian bloke sitting on a desk, clutching a long sword. Around him stood a few other guys holding knives. Then Es noticed a tall guy in a bomber jacket standing in the corner. He was pointing a gun.

"Big men, aren't you?" Es said, looking at each of them. "We've just come for a talk. Why do you need swords, knives and guns? We haven't come tooled up. If you want a row, let's have one."

"What do you think you're doing coming to our manor?" barked the Asian guy. "Who do you think you are?"

"One of our blokes was beaten up and we've come to sort it. That's all," Es said, thinking that he didn't sound very convincing.

He felt something cold being placed against the side of his temple. Out of the corner of his eye, he saw that it was a gun. The hands of the guy holding it were visibly shaking. This was it, Es thought. He was going to be shot. He knew that he had to front it out and not let them know how frightened he was.

"Come on, then. Let's have a row," Es said, trying not to show any fear.

John looked at Es as if to say, "Es, what are you doing? Shut your mouth."

"Look, there's seven of you and two of us," said Es, opening the palms of his hands. He sensed that the bloke with the gun was out of control. His finger was on the trigger and he was still shaking. 'Any second now,' he thought to himself, 'he's going to pull that trigger.'

The door opened and he was amazed to see a familiar face standing there. It was Bob Farlow, the ex-manager at the Penthouse club. Es hadn't seen him for several years. Bob stood in the doorway, looking shocked.

"What's going on here?" he demanded. "Put those tools down."

"They've come to our manor looking for trouble, and they've found it," said the Asian guy, sliding off the desk.

"Listen, Bob, we're here because Robert has had liberties taken with him. We've just come over for a chat. We just want to sort it one way or the other," said Es, hoping that Bob didn't find the cosh.

Farlow ignored him and pointed to the door. "Escort them out of the club, but don't harm them."

John and Es were then led out of the office and across the dance floor, which had now begun to fill up with punters. People stared, clearly wondering what was happening. As they were pushed outside, one of the bouncers shouted, "And don't come back! Stay on your own manor."

The street outside was swarming with Old Bill. Es's first thought was to find out what had happened to the other guys. What were those shots?

"Es, why did you keep winding up that bloke with the gun?" asked John, as they headed towards where the car was parked.

"I thought it was the best way to handle the situation."

"Well, you nearly got us killed, mate."

Two of the firm then appeared, looking shaken. "We had to run like hell," said one of them.

"Those blokes at the club began firing everywhere," said the other. "I hid behind a car."

"Yeah, I had to dive into someone's garden," said the first one. "I didn't expect this lot to have shooters."

"If Bob Farlow hadn't arrived, I'd have been shot and my body put in a bin liner and dumped somewhere," said Es.

In bed that night, Es's mind wandered back over events at the club. He could still feel the cold steel pressed to his temple – he was so close to being killed. Who had tipped them off? It must have been that barmaid Robert knew. Who else could it be? Robert had probably bragged to her that he had arranged for some guys from east London to come over and sort it out.

Rumours soon started to circulate that the Ealing firm were going to come over to Fairlop Waters the following Wednesday. Es began to assemble a team, making sure this time that some of them had shooters. He collected a handgun from a guy he knew in Manor Park. Early on Wednesday evening, Es and his firm arrived at Fairlop Waters expecting a tear-up. He plotted the guys in strategic positions. Several were positioned upstairs with guns, while others sat in the bar or in cars in the car parks on either side of the drive, looking out for any strange behaviour, such as blokes getting out of their car and opening the boot. But the other firm didn't turn up.

*   *   *

Es was still doing what was called 'debt collecting'. It was lucrative work, and the bigger the debt, the more Es got paid.

One evening, he went with one of his doormen to a flat on a council estate on the Isle of Dogs to recover some money owed to a guy who ran a furniture shop. They parked up near a vandalised phone box and made their way towards the entrance, where a group of youths in baseball caps and tracksuits were loitering. The youths eyed them suspiciously as they passed by. Es glared back at them and continued on to the lift, which was covered in graffiti.

They got out on the sixth floor and walked along the balcony to the flat. One pane of the kitchen window had been replaced by a wooden board. Es rang the bell and waited. He heard raised voices from another flat somewhere. No one came to the door, but he could hear the sound of the TV from inside the flat. Ringing the bell again, he then bent down and peered through the letter-box. "Come on! Open the door!" he shouted through it.

"Shall we kick it in?" asked the doorman, slipping on his knuckle-duster.

Es nodded, then took two steps back and launched a flying kick at the door. It flew open and they stormed into the living room. Sitting on the settee was a terrified-looking young black woman cradling a crying baby.

"Don't hurt me! He ain't here," she sobbed, rocking the baby.

"Where is he?"

"I dunno, man . . . He ain't been here since Monday. Honest."

Es looked around at the peeling walls, scruffy carpet and battered furniture. In the kitchen, he could see a filthy-looking cooker and a sink full of dirty saucepans and dishes. An aroma of fish hung in the air. He checked the bedroom and the bathroom, but they were both empty.

"Come on, let's go," he said sharply to the

doorman, turning around and walking back out.

"What's up?" he asked Es once they got outside.

"I'm through with this sort of stuff, mate. It's good money, but it's not my scene."

∗　∗　∗

One evening, Es received a phone call from one of his door staff, who was working at a disco in the Beacon Leisure Centre in Dagenham. The door was being run by Matthew Thomas. The previous week, after their regular Sunday morning game of football for Ferns in Seven Kings, Matthew had asked him to supply extra staff, as trouble was anticipated.

"Es, it's all going to kick off," he said.

"What do you mean?"

"There's two big groups of blokes here and they're getting ready for a tear-up."

"How many of them are there?"

"I reckon there must be about two hundred of them. There's only ten of us. We need back-up."

Es thought quickly. "Okay, leave it with me. I'll get some guys together and we'll be over there straight away."

He phoned Louis and all his available door staff, and told them to get to the leisure centre straight away. Slipping a cosh into his pocket, he got into his car and set off for the leisure centre. Parking his car, he was surprised to see that several police vans and cars were parked outside. The Old Bill had clearly decided to sit it out, rather than risk getting injured if it kicked off. Within half an hour, Louis and around sixty doormen had arrived there.

"Not sounding too good in there," said Es to Matthew when he arrived.

Matthew shook his head solemnly. "I'm going to have a word with the ring leaders." Matthew was a martial arts expert who, at one time, had been the country's top kick boxer, and he had also been one of the founders of West Ham United's notorious Inter City Firm (ICF). He was well known in the area and had a lot of respect.

Es and Louis followed Matthew into the leisure centre, which was heaving with revellers. Es could feel the tension in the air. 'If this goes off,' he thought to himself, 'it's going to be carnage.' The sixty doormen took up positions around the walls and at the bar.

"Make sure you don't get in front of me. Stay tucked in behind," said Matthew, as they threaded their way through the crowd.

Es watched as Matthew walked up to a group of guys and began speaking to them. Suddenly Matthew whipped out a plastic container from his pocket and squirted it at them. Three guys staggered back, clutching their faces, while the others backed away. Matthew then turned nonchalantly around and walked away.

"What's the outcome?" asked Es, already knowing the answer.

"Sorted, Es," replied Matthew with a grin.

* * *

By now, Es had got to know members of some of London's major criminal firms and he knew where and how to get hold of virtually anything, including guns, fake driving licences and MOTs, and cheap booze and cigarettes. Often this just involved a visit to certain pubs in the East End. But he never felt that he wanted to get involved in more serious crime such as armed robbery and drug dealing. He had never sought a reputation, unlike some guys he knew, but now that he had one, he had to protect it because it was his livelihood. One afternoon, he was driving along Silvertown Way with one of his door staff, on the way to visit a fortune-teller who lived above an off-licence in Canning Town. His fascination with fortune-tellers had rubbed off on Es.

"You know what, Es?" he said thoughtfully.

"What?"

"You've got a real reputation around Ilford now."

"Yeah, I suppose I have," replied Es, looking up at a small plane from London City Airport climbing high into the clear blue sky above Royal Albert Dock. He was aware that he'd built up a reputation in the Ilford area as a hard man, and the fact that he was known to sometimes carry guns only added to this. But he only ever carried a gun, usually a 9mm automatic pistol, when he thought a situation might demand it.

"If you teamed up with a couple of the other firms you could probably run London."

"You reckon?" replied Es, absentmindedly scanning the bleak-looking tower blocks, factories and industrial wasteland in what had once been the docks.

"Yeah. Think about it. You'd be very powerful. And think of the money. You could pull in thousands."

Over the next few weeks, Es thought about what the doorman had said. Although he had never wanted to become a major criminal, he had to admit that the idea of making big money was tempting, now that Aaron, his third child, had been born. But was it worth the risk of a prison sentence?

Richard Pryor and Es demonstrating 'control
and restraint techniques' during a training
course for Door Supervisors.

With Gary Lucy of the pop group Blue.

Chapter Six

Left for Dead

Es Kaitell had never seen Scouse Pete so angry; so angry that he was slamming the ashtray on the bar as he spoke. It took Es a good few minutes to calm him down.

"Those effing blokes over the road!" fumed Scouse Pete, pointing out of the window of the Havelock, a packed, smoky pub in High Road, Ilford. It was a Monday night in February 1992, and many of those in the pub were tanking up before going across the road to the Palais.

Es had heard on the grapevine that Pete was coming back to act the relief at the Havelock. A well-built guy with a typical Liverpuddlian sense of humour, Pete always had a one-liner and could easily have been a stand-up comic. Es thought he looked a bit like the big guy in the Hale and Pace comedy duo, whose take-off of doormen – 'the management' – was very popular on TV at the time. Pete had once worked for Es on the doors a few years before and had also run

Pickwick's wine bar in Ilford until moving up to Yorkshire, where he'd gone to train as a publican with Taylor Walker.

"Go on," said Es, leaning closer.

"Those bouncers at the Palais. Me and Julia were queuing up to go in when one of them asked to search her. I didn't mind – I've worked the doors and I know the score. We weren't out for trouble, just a nice evening. But the girl who was searching her took ages and then tipped her handbag onto the floor, for no reason."

"That's right," interrupted Julie, his wife. "They've no right to do that."

Es nodded sympathetically. He didn't like to see anyone being bullied.

"Yeah. So I asked them what they were playing at, and they just laughed. Then about half a dozen of them came over and one of them said, 'Get out and take your effing slag with you.'"

"You what?" Es was becoming more and more incensed as he listened to Scouse Pete's story.

Pete shook his head. "The bastards! No one treats me like that."

"Right," said Es, putting his drink down. "Let's go over there and have a word."

Two of Es's mates, Chunky, a small, quiet guy, and Crazy Joe, a flamboyant West Indian with a neatly trimmed goatee beard, came up to him.

"Problem, Es?" asked Chunky.

"I've got to go and have a chat with someone."

"We'll come with you," said Crazy Joe.

Pete told Julie to go and wait for him in Bon Appetite, a nearby late-night takeaway run by Ahmed, a cheerful Turkish Cypriot. Es called Bon Appetite his HQ because he and Louis used to meet in a small room at the back with their door staff at the end of a night to have a drink and a kebab. Es, Pete, Chunky and Crazy Joe then left the Havelock and walked across the road towards the Palais. Seeing them coming, the five doormen standing on the steps, chatting among themselves, formed a line and took up an aggressive stance.

"Right, what's all this, lads?" Es said, standing halfway up the steps and motioning behind him to Scouse Pete. "What's been going on?"

"What you on about?" sneered a doorman with close-cropped hair, carelessly flicking his cigarette.

"My mate and his bird have been insulted by you lot."

"Yeah, you're the one," accused Pete.

"Is that right?" said a sly-looking doorman with short hair.

"Yeah, that's right. And you lot need to apologise."

"Get lost," said a stocky, blond doorman.

"Yeah, push off," said another.

"No one talks to my wife like that," screamed Pete, moving towards them.

"Leave it, Pete," said Es, placing a hand on his arm. He could see that this was going nowhere – the doormen weren't listening.

"You bastards!" swore Pete. "You won't get away with this."

"Pete, come on," Es said calmly, moving back down the steps.

Reluctantly, Pete followed him and they headed over the road to Bon Appetite.

"Okay, Es?" smiled Ahmed from behind the counter. "You don't look too happy, my friend."

"Yeah, bit of business to sort out, Ahmed."

He nodded knowingly. "Well, go on through and I'll be with you in a minute. Your friend's lady's already there."

They made their way into the back room, where Julia was sitting anxiously at a table.

While Pete, Chunky and Crazy Joe were talking about the attitude of the bouncers, Es made an excuse and slipped back out. Scowling and with his adrenaline pumping, he headed back across the road to the Palais. He bounded up the steps, pushing past a couple of punters who were standing chatting, shoved open the doors, strode into the foyer and made for the stairs, thinking that's where he'd find the bouncers who had insulted Pete's missus. Having once worked the doors at the Palais, he knew the layout of the club well.

"Oi! Where do you think you're going?" shouted a voice.

Ignoring this, Es ran up the stairs. He had only one thing on his mind: to get an apology. It was as if he was on auto-pilot. As it was only 9.30 pm, the Palais wasn't that busy, and the sound of 'Goodnight Girl' by Wet Wet Wet drifted up from the dance floor below.

Reaching the top of the stairs, he pushed open the double doors and saw the bouncer with close-cropped hair standing at the bottom of a flight of steps with his back to the wall. Seeing Es, he froze, and then immediately slipped his right hand inside his jacket. Es knew what this meant, so he leapt towards him, grabbing his jacket lapels, while at the same time shoving him through a set of double doors. The bouncer stumbled back onto the steps that led to the office.

"Now, listen! Tomorrow, you go to the Havelock and you apologise to Pete and his wife," Es said, as he pinned him to the floor.

The bouncer struggled to get free, so Es put more body weight on him and grabbed his neck with his right hand. "Do you hear me? You'll go to the Havelock tomorrow and apologise to my mate. Got it?"

"Aagh! Let go!" he squealed, as Es gripped his neck more tightly.

"You going to apologise, then?"

"Get lost!" The guy struggled furiously, but Es was too strong for him.

"No?" Es gripped his neck even more tightly and said sternly, "You are going to apologise."

"All right! Aagh! I'll apologise to her. But not to him."

"Good," said Es, releasing his grip and standing up. Es knew that what had made Scouse Pete angry was that his wife had been insulted. Having worked on the doors, he was used to being insulted, but he didn't like someone taking liberties with his wife.

"Make sure you do," Es warned, turning around and pushing through the double doors.

As he did, he was confronted by three massive blokes, wearing long coats. He stopped dead in his tracks, wondering what to do. They stood facing each other for a moment. Es could see what looked like the dark, shiny end of a baseball bat protruding from the coat of the one in the middle. 'I bet they've all got baseball bats,' he thought, cursing inwardly. 'I should have come tooled up.'

He then heard the doors squeak open behind him, and out of the corner of his eye he saw the guy he'd just had pinned down on the floor standing there.

"Let's see who's the tough guy now," said a bloke with slicked-back hair, tapping a baseball bat gently against his leg.

"Yeah, you shouldn't stick your nose in where it doesn't concern you," said someone else.

"I don't like my mates being insulted," said Es, his heart racing.

"Tough," grunted the guy behind him.

Es quickly considered his options. He knew he was trapped. What were his chances of fighting his way out? True, he was 6' 5", strong and muscular, but he was up against four blokes, and three of them had bats; he knew they meant business. But he wasn't going down without a fight, that was for sure.

He pulled his fist back and slammed it into the face of the bloke immediately in front of him, knocking him sideways.

"Right! Let's do him," shouted someone.

In a flash, the others leapt on him and began laying into him with baseball bats. He struggled to get free, while trying to protect himself by covering his head with his arms, but as strong as he was he was no match for the four blokes. Blows rained down on his head, back and legs. Bam! Bam! Bam! He felt his head begin to pound and blood oozing down his face and from his mouth. It was as if the life was being sucked out of him. Everything became a blur until, finally, he lost consciousness.

*　*　*

"Where am I?" moaned Es.

"You're in King George's Hospital," said a voice.

"King George's?" Es blinked and tried to take in the words. At the end of his bed he could make out the shape of a man in a white coat.

"That's right. You're going to have to have an operation. How are you feeling?"

"Rough," he groaned, trying to move his mouth.

"You've got some serious injuries," said the doctor.

"How serious?" Es replied, tenderly feeling his cheeks.

"You should be dead," said the doctor, shaking his head and then adding, "And if you hadn't been so big and strong, you probably would have been."

"Yeah?" These words sent a chill through Es. How come he might have ended up dead? What had happened? He tried to unscramble his thoughts, but his mind was a blur.

"You'll be okay, don't worry," continued the doctor in a more upbeat voice. "You're in safe hands now."

Es lay there in bed and slowly started to remember the events of the night before. Gradually they came back to him: the Havelock, Scouse Pete, going to the Palais, Bon Appetite, grappling with a bloke . . . and then the flurry of baseball bats.

The next morning, he underwent a seven-and-a-half-hour operation, during which his head was opened up and two metal plates inserted, and a plastic spacer was put underneath his left eye.

Afterwards, the consultant said gravely, "I have to tell you that if you get hit on the left side of your temple, it could be fatal."

Es was discharged a week later. He felt dreadful, but was relieved to be going home. There was no sign of Carron and baby Aaron when he opened the front door. She was probably staying at her mum's, he guessed. She had taken to regularly disappearing for days at a time.

The next day, he was lying on the settee watching TV when he heard a key turn in the door and then the sound of baby Aaron crying.

"Es, what's happened to you?" said Carron, alarmed.

When he told her about the attack, she adopted a sympathetic tone. "Well, you've got to take it easy."

"Yeah, I know. There's not much I can do in this state."

"Well, at least you'll be at home for once now," she said, her tone suddenly changing.

A couple of days later, Louis phoned. "How are you, mate?"

"Bearing up. But I ain't going to make the Olympic team this year," he replied, and then briefly described his injuries.

"I've heard on the grapevine that the bouncer you pinned to the floor smashed a knuckle duster into your face when you were lying on the floor unconscious."

"Who told you that?"

"I heard it from Chunky."

When Es heard this, anger welled up inside of him. Right, he decided, that was it. He was going to make these guys pay for what they did.

Over the next few days, a number of people phoned, asking how he was and whether he wanted them to sort out the blokes who had attacked him. By now, Es had not only found out their names but also where they lived. They were surprised when he told them to leave it. He knew that he would have to wait until he was physically fit again before exacting his revenge. He would make sure these guys suffered more than he had.

The pains in his head were unbearable, despite the

four daily painkillers. They helped to ease the pain but didn't remove it entirely. Some days his head felt like a volcano about to explode. When it got hot, the metal in his head would expand. This sometimes happened when he got angry. His left eye was very watery and he had blurred vision. One of the things he missed most was eating steak and chips, fry-ups and all the food he was used to. He couldn't clamp his teeth together properly, so he could neither chew nor bite. Instead, he had to drink through straws, all his food was liquidised. The pain was excruciating.

He became like a prisoner in his own home. When he woke up in the morning, he would lie there in bed for ages, trying to get his mind working and summon some enthusiasm to face the day. The only time he ventured out was to go to the newsagent at the corner of the street. He often felt dizzy. He would sit in an armchair in the living room, listening to his Luther Vandross and George Benson tapes to try and take his mind off the pain. At times, he felt that he was clinging to life with his fingertips. Part of him wanted to be alive; the other part didn't. It was only his three children that kept him going and his desire for revenge.

One morning, after a restless night in bed, he went into the kitchen, where Carron was ironing Aaron's clothes. Sitting down at the table, he said, "Carron, I don't know if I can take much more of this."

"I know what you must be going through."

"I've even thought about killing myself."

She put the iron down and stood in front of him. "Listen, if you kill yourself, what about Aaron? And what about Carl and Natalie?"

"Yeah, I know," he sighed. She was right, of course. He had to think of his kids. What would they do without him?

Louis and Andy managed to keep WK going. He was relieved about this, but it didn't ease the frustration he felt at not being able to work.

One morning, Joe, a well-known face from the north-east of England. phoned, Es had first met him at Redworth Hall some years before.

"I've heard about what happened. They gave you a right going over by the sounds of it," he said.

"Too true, mate. I'm lucky to be alive."

"Do you want them taken out?" he asked darkly, as if it was the most natural thing in the world. Joe ran a heavy-duty firm involved in everything from protection rackets to running nightclubs and buying and selling dodgy gear. They wouldn't think twice about bumping off those blokes if that was what he wanted. They would probably carry out a drive-by shooting.

"No. Leave it." Es saw the attack as personal, and didn't want anyone else fighting his battles. He wanted to deal with these guys himself – when the time was right; he was prepared to wait patiently.

"Well, if you change your mind, give us a call. We'll come down straight away, Es. You know that."

Much of his life now seemed to revolve around sitting in hospital departments, waiting to see some doctor or other. At the end of June, he went to see Mr Coughlan, a consultant at the London Hospital.

"I've had this pain for four-and-a-half months, and I can't go on. I'm going to top myself. You have to do something for me," he pleaded.

Mr Coughlan nodded sympathetically. "Well, we can take the metal plates out and put them in a more comfortable position, but the left side of your face might be paralysed. We can take the plastic spacer out from underneath your eye and resite it. You can have the lower jaw reset to enable you to chew, but it might break again. Alternatively, we can put you on the strongest painkillers we have for an indefinite period. You need to make up your mind quickly though."

Es left the hospital feeling more depressed than before. The situation was hopeless. He didn't want his head opened up again and run the risk of paralysis and he didn't want to risk his jaw breaking again. But neither did he want to be taking painkillers for the rest of his life.

After a few weeks, he decided to walk to Stopouts early one evening. He wanted to see his mates for a chat and to catch up on what had been happening on the manor. He was fed up with being at home all day. Nearing the Palais, he saw a couple of doormen quickly disappear back inside. As he walked past, several police cars suddenly appeared. The bouncers had phoned the Old Bill. He carried on walking, deliberately avoiding eye contact with the Old Bill, secretly pleased that the bouncers were worried. They had every right to be.

Worryingly, he began to develop short-term memory loss. Before the attack, he was like a walking phone book: people would ask him a number and he could tell them straight away. Now he couldn't remember anyone's phone number.

One Tuesday morning, Ian McDowell came to see Es to discuss the future of Southern Court, a licensed debt-collecting service they had set up together. Ian felt that they should be bringing more money in. But sitting at the desk in his loft, listening to Ian talking about plans to advertise the company in local newspapers, Es's mind began to wander, and he found himself staring absentmindedly at the calendar on the wall.

"You okay, Es?" Ian asked with concern.

"Sorry, mate, I can't take it in. It's my head."

"Let's leave it until you're feeling better then," Ian said, standing up.

"I think you're right, mate," Es replied.

Ian promised to ring the following week before making his way down the metal steps to the landing. His head then reappeared and he called, "Will you come to church?" As he said this, he took a step back.

Church? Was Ian a Christian, then? He'd never mentioned it and Es would never have guessed. For some reason, he found himself replying, "Yeah, okay." He hadn't been to church since he was a kid, because he had found it meaningless and boring.

"You will?" Ian said, surprised.

"Yeah," Es repeated, still wondering what he was saying.

Ian explained that he went to a church in Canning Town each week with his wife Val and daughter Bianca. He agreed to pick up Es at ten o'clock on Sunday.

"Yeah, okay, mate."

After Ian had gone, Es sat there wondering why he had agreed to go to church. He didn't even believe in God. No, he'd make up an excuse to get out of going. He'd think of something.

Chapter Seven

The Road to Notting Hill

The church was called Elim Way Fellowship and it turned out to be in the hall of a primary school in Canning Town. As Es walked in, a man in a suit came over to him and shook his hand warmly. "Nice to see you," he smiled.

Es looked at him, wondering why he seemed so friendly. He found himself thinking that the warmth generated was in stark contrast to the dark feelings swirling round inside him. He smiled thinly and followed Ian into the school. They took their seats in the hall and waited for the service to begin. Looking around, Es was surprised by the variety of people that were there: black, white, Asian, young, old, children, all sorts. A simple cross stood on a small table at the front of the hall. The walls were decorated with brightly coloured children's paintings and animal posters.

Eventually, a man in a suit appeared on the stage and everyone began singing a hymn. The man then spoke for quite a long time, quoting passages from the

Bible. Es couldn't understand what he was on about. The guy might as well have been speaking Chinese for all the sense it made.

After the service Ian asked, "What did you think, Es? Did you like it?"

"Yeah, it was okay," Es shrugged.

"Are you coming next week?"

Es nodded, even though he didn't really understand the service. For some reason his internal hatred and anger seemed to have diminished.

He attended the church the following three Sundays and felt a little bit brighter each time he went, but he still wanted to extact his revenge. He knew that since the attack the Old Bill had put him under surveillance. Louis and himself had a reputation in and around Ilford, and he reckoned that the Old Bill feared a gang war.

One afternoon, as he pulled up outside his flat in Empress Avenue, a Vauxhall Astra stopped behind him. 'This looks like the Old Bill,' he thought, studying the man and the woman getting out of the car and walking towards him.

"Police," said the woman. "Did you know that you made an illegal turn back there?"

"An illegal turn? What do you mean?" he demanded. He knew he hadn't made any illegal turns, so what was this about?

"When you turned off the Drive."

"No, I didn't," Es replied sharply. He knew he was being goaded.

The male officer then produced his two-way radio and started giving details of Es's car to the control centre. After a minute or so, he said, "Okay. On your way."

Feeling annoyed, Es slammed his car door shut and stormed into the flat. He hated the Old Bill.

After the church service the following Sunday, Marcus, Ian's brother-in-law and also a doorman, asked, "Do you want to come to a prophetic conference next week, Es?"

"What?"

"A prophetic conference."

"What's that?" Es didn't have a clue what he was going on about.

"It's church, but with a minister who is a prophet. There's an American preacher coming to the Kensington Temple in Notting Hill."

What had he got to lose? "Okay, yeah. When is it?"

"It's on Monday evening."

"You'd better remind me nearer the time, I might forget," Es responded.

The Sunday afternoon before the conference, Es was sitting at home watching TV when, without warning, the hearing in his left ear seemed to go. Frightened, he got up and went straight to the bathroom to examine himself in the mirror. He twisted his head this way and that, but his ears still looked normal.

"Carron! Carron!" he yelled. "What's happening?"

She came running out of the bedroom. "What's the matter, Es?"

He could just about make out her words. "There's something up with my hearing," he shouted, shaking his head.

She urged him to go and lie down for a while. He did as she suggested, and it was at this point that he made up his mind: these blokes who were the cause of all his suffering were going to die. He would phone the firm in the north-east.

The next morning, while he was getting his breakfast, a searing pain shot through his right leg. It was excruciating. It had eased a little by the afternoon, but he was worried that he might have to stand at the conference since Marcus had told him this preacher often attracted big crowds. He was in two minds whether or not to go, but he didn't want to let Marcus down.

Later that evening, he and Carron met Marcus and his wife outside Gants Hill Underground station to catch the Central Line to Notting Hill Gate on the other side of London.

"All set, Es?" asked Marcus chirpily.

"Yeah, mate, but I've had some really bad pains in my leg today and my hearing's not too good. I was in two minds about turning up today."

"I'll tell you, Es, God uses this preacher in a special way. I've seen an old lady get up out of her wheelchair and walk; I've seen people's legs grow. Real miracles. Jesus is alive today, mate."

"Seriously?" Es wasn't sure what to make of all this. Did Marcus think he had 'mug' written across his forehead? But he didn't say anything, as he didn't want to cause offence.

On the train, they chatted about this and that for a while, then Marcus turned to Es and said with a serious look, "You know, Es, you've got to forgive those blokes who attacked you."

"What do you mean, forgive them?" Es snapped back, causing startled looks from several people in the carriage. When Marcus had said the word 'forgive' it was as if he'd hit him on the head with a hammer. "I'm lucky to be alive. They beat the living daylights out of me, so don't talk to me about forgiveness," he said angrily.

Marcus nodded. "I know, but you have to forgive."

"Why should I?" Es interrupted, his voice rising. It was all right for Marcus to go spouting on about forgiveness and all that stuff. He hadn't been beaten senseless and made to suffer like Es had. Why was he siding with the blokes at the Palais?

"You have to understand the ways of God, mate. If you don't forgive, God won't forgive you."

"If there is a God, then he probably won't forgive me anyway, considering some of the things I've done," Es retorted, wanting to hit Marcus.

"He will, Es. That's why he died on the cross. He paid the price for our sins, but we have to forgive, even when it's really hard."

"It's not as easy as that, Marcus. I'll tell you what, forgiveness is the last thing on my mind at the moment. Revenge is what I want. Doesn't the Bible talk about an eye for an eye and a tooth for a tooth?"

"Yeah, but Jesus told us that we have to forgive each other. If we do this, he'll give us a fresh start."

Es said nothing for the rest of the journey – he couldn't bring himself to talk to Marcus. When the train slid into Oxford Circus station and the doors opened, he thought about getting off, but something told him not to. By the time they came up out of Notting Hill Gate Underground station, Es was seething. It was easy for Marcus to talk about forgiveness, but how would he feel if he was in the same situation? They crossed at the traffic lights by W. H. Smith and walked in silence towards a large building. From the large knots of people milling around outside, Es guessed this must be Kensington Temple.

As they walked towards the entrance, a strange thing happened. To Es's amazement, the anger in him suddenly subsided and he found himself forgiving the blokes who had beaten him up. He felt puzzled and uneasy, but didn't say anything to the others. They squeezed through the crowded foyer and ended up in a large hall with a balcony above. The place was packed and buzzing with conversation. They found four seats towards the back and sat down. Looking around, Es thought to himself, 'I don't belong here. I should go.'

"All right, Es?" asked Marcus, turning towards him.

"Yeah," he lied, wishing he hadn't agreed to come.

Then he heard music start up and the words to a hymn appeared on a large screen above the stage.

People around him began singing rhythmically, raising their arms in the air. Seeing that some of the blokes near him were crying, Es thought this was ridiculous. What were grown men crying for? Then a casually dressed man in a neat beard and with piercing eyes, together with a young woman, appeared on the stage, smiling. The man took hold of a microphone and waited for the song to finish.

"The Spirit of the Lord is here tonight," he began in an American accent. Standing behind him, the woman began singing softly and gently swaying. Some people cheered and started excitedly calling out the name of Jesus.

"The Spirit of the Lord is telling me about a man who had a motorcycle accident a couple of years ago. Well, the Lord's going to heal him tonight. And there's a woman who needs her tailbone fixing. The Lord will heal her, too."

Cries of 'alleluia' interrupted the speaker. Some people raised their arms in the air and started praying out loud.

"There's also someone here tonight who was severely beaten up six months ago," continued the preacher. "The Lord's telling me that he has head pains, has blurred vision, can't eat properly and sometimes he wishes he was dead. Well, he too is going to be healed by the power of Jesus tonight."

'This sounds like me,' Es thought to himself. 'But it can't be.' The preacher didn't know him and he knew that neither Marcus, his wife nor Carron had spoken to him. Es sat transfixed as the preacher continued. 'This is uncanny,' he thought.

"Now, I want anyone who has an injury to stand up," the preacher called out.

All around the hall people began standing up. Es hesitated and then, slowly, found himself doing as the preacher asked, but he felt very foolish and thought that everyone was probably staring at him.

"You! The young black dude at the back." He seemed to be looking at Es. "The Lord thanks you for forgiving, son."

Es was stunned. How on earth could he know this?

"The Lord is going to heal you tonight," he went on confidently, raising his voice and pacing backwards and forwards on the stage.

Questions raced through Es's head. Was God real, then? Could he heal? Was what Marcus said true? But if all the doctors he'd seen couldn't heal him, how could this Jesus whom he couldn't see, hear or touch? He didn't know what to make of it all.

"Do not listen to the lies of Satan. You will not be paralysed. The Lord is going to heal you tonight," continued the preacher.

As he said this, Es's right leg began to shake. Then his whole body began to shake, and there was nothing he could do to stop it. An intense heat began to take over his body, especially his head. It was like being in a sauna, only hotter. To his horror, Es noticed wet patches had appeared on the front of his trousers, under his arm pits and on his shirt front, but he was filled with an incredible peace. All his pains, tensions, anger and awkwardness evaporated. He felt completely at one with himself. He'd never experienced anything like this in his entire life. It was amazing. When he sat back down, baffled by what had just happened, his pains returned. People started coming up to him and praying out loud and placing their hands on his shoulder.

He turned to Carron and whispered, "I fancy a coffee."

"Okay, Es," she replied, getting up.

They made their way to the foyer, where there was a vending machine. Carron put some coins in and handed him a cup of coffee, along with a packet of crisps. Opening the crisps, he put one in his mouth and, as usual, because he couldn't chew, began to suck it. Carron then offered him a biscuit. Es looked at her. Why had she given him a biscuit when she knew how difficult it was for him to eat biscuits. He was about to tell her off, but instead he took the biscuit and bit into it. He didn't feel any pain. He began to slowly move his jaw around and open his eyes wider. For the first time in six months, he could see clearly, the pains in his head had subsided, and he felt what seemed like a power surge through his stomach. Deep inside he knew that this Jesus he'd been told about had healed him. Marcus and the preacher in Canning Town had talked about him as Healer, Saviour and Deliverer. Now he could understand what they meant. Returning to his seat he joined in the singing, following the unfamiliar words on the screen. He became aware of a terrible, putrid smell. Embarrassed, he looked around at the other people and thought, I bet they think it's me. He knew it couldn't be him, because he'd had a bath that afternoon. But judging from the facial expressions of the people around him, it seemed that no one else could smell it.

"Don't worry if your body smells right now. The Lord is purging your system," said the preacher all of a sudden. "Now, all those who don't know Jesus and who want to, raise your hand and stand up."

Along with a couple of dozen or so other people scattered around the hall, Es stood up.

"Now, recite these words after me," began the preacher. "Lord Jesus, I invite you into my life."

Es repeated the words after the preacher. He asked God for forgiveness for his sins and then thanked him for saving him. When he came out of Kensington Temple, his head was still spinning with what he had just experienced. All his pains had disappeared, and he felt eighteen again.

"You okay, mate?" grinned Marcus, playfully slapping his back.

"Yeah, mate," he laughed. "I feel like a new man."

Es started attending Elim Way Fellowship each Sunday, going to prayer meetings, reading the Bible Ian McDowell had given him, and listening to Christian tapes. As he knew nothing about Christianity, he had a lot to learn. He found reading the Bible daunting at first until someone advised him to see it as a collection of books written at different times rather than a single volume. He found the book of Proverbs very easy to understand because it addressed everyday issues such as relationships, money and anger. And when he began reading the Acts of the Apostles he found that he could identify with Peter, whom he saw as a hard man who always seemed to be putting his foot in it, and Paul, who had been persecuting Christians before dramatically encountering God on the road to Damascus. Es felt that he had undergone a similar experience to Paul. When he came to read about Jesus in the gospels he saw him as an action figure, healing people and challenging religious leaders. He was struck by the words in John's gospel: "For God loved the world so much that he gave his only Son, so that everyone who believes in him may not die but have eternal life." 'Jesus died for me,' he said to himself, letting the words slowly sink in.

Es returned to the London Hospital for an appointment with Mr Coughlan. Driving along Mile End Road, he wondered how he would explain what had happened at the Kensington Temple. He decided not to mention that Jesus had healed him.

"So what have you decided? What are you going to do? asked Mr Coughlan.

"Nothing."

"What do you mean, nothing?"

"I'm not in any pain now."

"No pain?"

"That's right."

"Could you open your mouth for me?"

Es did as he was asked.

"Can you open it and close it?"

Again, Es did as he was asked.

Mr Coughlan then did further tests on Es's hearing and sight. At the end, he looked at Es in disbelief. "Well, it looks like there's nothing we can do."

"That's right," said Es.

As soon as Es left the hospital, he felt a heaviness descend on him and he knew that he should have told Mr Coughlan the truth. "Jesus," he prayed silently, "I'll never be quiet about you again. I know you're real and I know you're alive. I'll go where you want me to go and do what you want me to do."

Soon after, he was baptised at Balaam Street Baths in Plaistow, in front of a couple of hundred people sitting around the pool. He descended the steps into the water and stood between two Elim Way Fellowship elders. He confessed Jesus as his Saviour.

"We now baptise you in the name of the Father, the Son and the Holy Spirit," said one of the elders. Es was then gently lowered backwards into the water and then brought sharply back up in order to symbolise Christ's death and resurrection. Shaking the water from him and climbing back up the steps, Es felt elated.

It had been nine months since he had worked on the doors. As he now felt physically and emotionally strong enough, he decided to return, even though the doctor had warned him about the vulnerability of his temple. He knew that as a Christian, he would have to run his business differently. He would have to curb his aggression when faced with awkward punters. This wouldn't be easy, but he would trust in God to give him self-control.

One Sunday morning at Elim Way Fellowship in Canning Town, while chatting, a school teacher approached Es and said with disdain in his voice, "I hear that you are a bouncer."

"That's right," replied Es.

"Well, you can't be a Christian if you're a bouncer," the man replied stiffly and then walked off.

Es didn't know what to say. The guy was right – Christianity was about peace, not violence. He was troubled. He was attempting the impossible, given some of the pubs and clubs where he worked. He would put his faith in God. Es took consolation from the book of Zecharaiah: "You will succeed not by military might or by your own strength, but by my Spirit."

Left to right: Pete Edwards, a friend, Keith Butler
and Andy Pohl: a group of doormen
(all ex-military).

Hughie, WK doorman and amateur boxer,
outside Es's office.

Chapter Eight

Trust

Needing more space, Es decided to rent an office above a dry cleaner's near Highams Park Station and, despite difficulties in the relationship, he and Carron got married, at Ilford Baptist Church.

This was the time Es took the decision to convene his team for the 'No tools' briefing (*see chapter one*). Soon enough this initiative was being put to the test. While Es was doing some paperwork in the office, he received a call from one of his doormen at the Havelock.

"Es, Jimmy Rollings has been trying to get in. We told him he was barred, but I think he might come back."

"Yeah, he is barred – he's a trouble-maker. Okay, I'm on my way." Es didn't like Rollings. He was loud, aggressive and a bully who had been known to torture people.

Es grabbed his leather jacket and was about to take his cosh out of the cupboard in the kitchen when he remembered what he had said to his door staff about not using tools. He stared at it for a moment and then quickly slipped it into his inside pocket and headed for his car.

The pub was packed. He took up a position at the main door with Keith Butler, a 6' 4" unlicensed boxer and former soldier. Sure enough, it wasn't long before Rollings, a muscular bloke with short dreadlocks, appeared.

"Sorry, mate, you can't come in," said Es, stepping in front of him to block his way.

"Why?" challenged Rollings.

"Because you're barred. Now, I'm asking you nicely."

"Yeah? Well, I'm coming in and you're not going to stop me."

"Yeah?" repeated Es, preparing himself for what he knew was about to happen.

Rollings then tried to head-butt Es, who blocked him with his right arm before swiftly executing a head-lock. The two of them struggled for a while until Es managed to drag Rollings away from the pub.

"I've told you that you're barred," he said, roughly pushing the guy away. "Now, don't come back."

"Just you wait," snarled Rollings, storming off down the street. A few minutes later, he reappeared with a big black guy in a long leather coat. Rollings lunged at Es with a six-inch knife. Es got him into a bear hug, but wasn't able to knock the knife from his hand. Then he felt a stinging blow on the left side of his temple. The black guy had caught him with a killer of a punch. For some reason, Es didn't even flinch. Instead, he just fixed the guy with a piercing stare. Unsure of what to do, the guy fled.

"We'll have you," warned Rollings, following him.

"After we've cleared the pub, we'll oblige you," said Es matter of factly. He'd had enough of Rollings.

It was about an hour later when Es saw Rollings walk towards a red BMW parked outside Pizza Hut. Several guys were standing around it. Rollings opened the boot and he and the other guys reached inside. Es guessed what he was doing. Rollings and the guys then set off towards the house where he lived around the corner.

After phoning several of his doormen and telling them they were needed at the Havelock, Es found a quiet corner of the pub and sat down. The consultant at King George's Hospital had told him that if he ever got hit on the left side of his temple, it would be fatal. That guy had caught him there with a powerful punch, but he was fine. He felt that God was telling him to trust in him, not in man, and that he wanted him to continue working on the doors.

"Lord, you know what's happening," he prayed. "What do I do? I've a job to do. I can't walk away." He sat there for a few minutes, expecting some sort of sign from God. Nothing happened.

When several of his door staff arrived, they left the pub together and made their way to Rollings' house. They saw a group of guys milling around outside, and

Rollings was standing there wielding a great big piece of wood. Es approached him with his fists outstretched and then quickly drew his cosh and a fight ensued. Suddenly, police sirens sounded in the distance. Everyone then scattered in different directions. Es raced to his car, parked in the road behind Harrison Gibson's department store, and sped away to Fairlop Waters. His doormen were already there.

"Es, what's up with your arm?" asked one of them when he walked in.

"What?" replied Es, holding his arm up.

"There's blood dripping from you."

Taking off his leather jacket, he saw that his shirt was soaked in blood. "How did that happen?"

"One of the blokes cut you with a baby machete."

Two days later, Es was in a busy pub in Dagenham when a face he knew came up to him at the bar.

"You'd better watch your back," he whispered.

"What do you mean?"

The face moved closer to him. "I hear that Rollings is going to try and shoot you."

"Straight up?"

The face nodded.

Es tried to take this news on board. What should he do? He knew that Rollings was stupid enough to take a shot at him.

"Do you want me to get you a piece?" asked the face, looking anxiously around the scattering of drinkers in the pub.

Es thought for a moment. "Yeah."

The face took out a notebook, tore out a piece of paper and scribbled down the address of a guy who ran a car spares business in Hackney. "Tell him I sent you."

"Cheers," replied Es, slipping the piece of paper into his pocket.

The following Sunday after the service at Elim Way Fellowship, Es went to speak to his pastor, John Barr.

"John, there's something worrying me."

"What is it, Es?"

"Well . . ." He struggled to find the words.

"Es, you can't shock me. I've been around. Tell me what's troubling you."

"I've been carrying a gun." Es then explained what had happened.

After he had finished, John said, "Look, Es, I've known people who have carried a gun, thinking that it would protect them, but then found that the trigger jammed when they tried to fire it. What you have to do is trust in God. He will protect you."

Es knew he was right. Just after midnight, he left home and drove to an area of factories, warehouses, electricity pylons and derelict land around the River Lea between Stratford and East India Dock Road. On the way, he listened to a Bible tape in which the speaker was explaining how God's grace works in ordinary situations. Parking his car outside an abandoned factory in a deserted rubbish-strewn street, Es got out and walked quickly towards the canal. Looking left and right, to make sure no one was watching, he then dropped the gun into the dark, still water below. "I've got to trust in you, Lord, from now on. I'll give you my word that I'll never carry a gun again."

Apart from a distant hum of traffic and a train rattling by somewhere, the night was quiet. Es stood for a moment, the rain beating down, and took stock of his life. Did he really want to continue working in security? Maybe now that he had a new life with God he should give it all up and do something else. "God, get me out of this game," he prayed. "Find me something else."

The following Friday night, Es was working on the doors at Fairlop Waters with John Whitman. Small and stocky, John was one of the country's top bodybuilders. For some reason, Es felt that he should speak to him about Jesus – something he'd never done before.

"You know, John, since I accepted Jesus into my life, I've felt completely different. I'm a new man. But I'm not perfect – far from it."

"Yeah?"

"Have you ever thought about Jesus?"

John shook his head and smiled. "I'm not the religious type. I've nothing against religion. It suits some people, but it's not for me."

"I'm not talking about religion, John. I'm talking about Jesus. He's as alive today as he was 2,000 years ago."

"I'm pleased you've found him, Es, but this Christianity thing isn't for me."

Then Es found himself saying, "I think you've got a curse on your life."

"What made you say that?" replied John, startled.

"I just think you have."

"Well, my ex-girlfriend's mum has been sticking pins in a doll that's supposed to be me."

"You need some prayer, mate."

"Prayer? What do you mean?"

"This sort of stuff can only be got rid of through prayer. I'll pray with you if you want. There's power in prayer when it's in the name of Jesus."

John shook his head. "Thanks, Es, but I don't think so."

"Fair enough, but if you change your mind at any point, give me a ring."

On Tuesday, under a grey east London sky, Es was driving along Heathway in Dagenham when his mobile phone rang. It was John Whitman. "Es, those things we were talking about."

"Yeah?"

"You said that you would pray with me if I wanted you to."

"That's right. I will."

"Well, I think I'd like you to."

"Okay, when do you want to meet?"

"How about Thursday?"

"Yeah, okay," replied Es. But as he ended the call he felt a bit uneasy.

A few minutes later, John rang back. "Where are you, Es?"

"In Dagenham, on my way to the Fort Galaxy gym to drop some wages off."

"Yeah? That's where I am now," said John.

"Well, I'll see you there in ten minutes."

"Okay, but don't say anything to the other blokes."

The Fort Galaxy gym was tucked away in a narrow lane behind the shops in High Road, Ilford. A lot of the WK door staff came here to work out or to play pool. John came out to meet Es.

"Okay, shall we pray?" asked Es brightly.

John looked puzzled. "What, here?"

"Yeah. God's everywhere. You don't have to go into a church to find him."

Es led him into the yard of the disused unit next to the gym, so as to be out of sight. Placing his hand on John's shoulder, Es said, "God will meet you at your point of need." Es knew that John had kidney and liver problems through taking a substance called Nubane to improve his performance as a bodybuilder, and that he had been having treatment with a specialist in Harley Street. "The Bible says that by Jesus' stripes we are healed. I'm going to ask for God to heal you." Es asked him to close his eyes to save him any embarrassment. "Jesus, you are the Healer. You've healed me and you've healed countless other people. I ask you to heal John. Amen."

John opened his eyes.

"John, you can throw away your medication now. Jesus has healed you."

"How do you know?"

"I just do. You'll be fine from now on."

A couple of days later an excited John phoned Es.

"I've no more pains and I'm not peeing blood any more!"

Es smiled to himself. "Keep praising Jesus, John. Keep thanking him. He's done it, not me."

"I'm going to go and buy a Bible from W. H. Smith."

Es felt humbled that John had listened to him talking about Jesus, but he knew that there were still many areas of his own life where he was falling short. One night, he was sitting with some of his doormen in Bon Appetite when Ahmed, the owner, said jovially, "Es, you've given up the booze, but I see you're still smoking weed."

"Yeah, mate. I find it relaxes me," replied Es, feeling a bit uncomfortable.

Ahmed chuckled and returned to the kitchen. Es felt troubled by what he had said. How could he justify taking drugs now that he was a Christian? He knew that he couldn't. Stubbing out the spliff in the ashtray, he prayed silently, "Lord, I need your power never to smoke weed again."

One afternoon, Es was in Gants Hill when he saw a stocky, shaven-headed guy in a blue tracksuit walking towards him. It was Alan Mortlock, for whom Es had supplied security at the international kick-boxing show at the Picketts Lock Centre in 1989.

"Hello, mate, how you doing?" said Alan, shaking his hand.

"Still in security," said Es. "What about you?"

"Well, you're not going to believe this, but I've given my life to Jesus. I'm a born-again Christian."

Es's eyes lit up. "And you're not going to believe this. So am I."

The two of them broke into laughter and went off to a nearby cafe to hear each other's story. Es came away from his encounter with Alan uplifted and marvelling at the way God works in people's lives. Like himself, Alan used to have a reputation on the streets, and on one occasion had been sent to prison for stabbing a guy in a brawl outside the Room at the Top in Ilford.

In the security business trouble was never far away. One morning, Es received a phone call from John Brown, the manager of Stopouts.

"Es, I need to see you urgently. Can you come over?"

"Sure, I'm on my way." Es jumped into his car and set off for Stopouts.

John ushered him into the back office. "Es, there's been meetings going on at the Chinatown restaurant. Be careful. What's going on isn't right."

"What are you talking about?"

"Alan, my business partner, has been having meetings with John the Kickboxer about him taking over this door and a few other doors."

"You serious?"

"Yeah."

Es was stunned. He considered John the Kickboxer a friend and he had known him since they worked together at the Penthouse all those years ago.

"Where do you stand?" asked Es.

"Well, Es, I like you and I want you to carry on

running the doors here, but Alan is the main partner . . . I'm sorry."

A dark mood descended over Es as he drove back home along Green Lane. He reckoned that John the Kickboxer was making a move on the door because Es had become a Christian and would therefore be a pushover. Well, Es might be a Christian, but he was no mug and he wasn't going to let John take liberties with him.

Later that day, he found out from Andy Pohl that John had approached the management at a number of other pubs and clubs where Es ran the doors and told them that Es had packed up security as a result of becoming a Christian and now the business was being handed over to them. Es felt betrayed. He would have put his life on the line for John and now he had gone behind his back to try and take over his doors.

The next day, Es contacted all the pubs and clubs he supplied with door staff and told the management that he wasn't packing up the business and that John the Kickboxer was trying to pull a fast one. He then phoned Matthew Thomas and asked him to set up a meet at Fairlop Waters.

"Sure, no problem, Es," said Matthew. "Let's sort this out."

"But I don't want anything to kick off, Matt. I'm a Christian now."

"I understand, mate. Don't worry."

On Sunday afternoon, Es drove to Fairlop Waters for a showdown. Es, Andy Pohl and Ian McDowell sat on one side of the table, with John, Alan Davies, the owner of Stopouts, and Claud Fontinelli, a doorman with WK, on the other. The atmosphere was very tense.

"Right," began Matthew in a business-like manner, "John, justify what you've done."

Looking at John and feeling the anger rising, Es prayed for self-control. John refused to look him in the eye. Instead, he just stared ahead at the wall.

"We thought Es was packing up," said John.

"Did he tell you that?" asked Matthew sharply.

"Well . . . not really, but . . ."

"But what?" cut in Matthew.

"Because he's become a Christian, we thought that he would be."

Es wasn't really listening to what John was saying. He was engulfed with anger and hatred for this betrayal. All he wanted to do was to beat John to a pulp for taking such a liberty with him, but he had to remind himself that he was now a Christian and he had to leave behind his old ways. God had saved him and forgiven him and he had to be loyal to him. He couldn't let him down.

Ian then stood up and said angrily, "John, you're lying and you know it."

Matthew then turned towards John and said with a fierce look, "Listen, mate, you've got Stopouts. But you don't go anywhere near Es's other doors. Got it?"

"Yeah," answered John meekly.

"I was really struggling there. I wanted to go for

John," said Es to Ian as they drove away from Fairlop Waters.

"Listen, Es, don't condemn yourself. We're Christians, but we're also people with emotions, mate. God understands. But you can't do it with your own strength. In 2 Corinthians 12:9 St Paul says that God told him, 'My grace is all you need, for my power is strongest when you are weak.'"

On the advice of his pastor, John Barr, Es went to see Eddie and Sylvie, a married Christian couple in Hornchurch, to talk about his childhood and also have counselling about issues in his life such as anger and self-control.

"So how did you feel about growing up in a white family?" asked Sylvie.

"I was loved at home, but outside I often felt rejected."

"Did you talk about this?"

"No, I kept my feelings in. I was quite shy as a kid."

"And do you think anger is sometimes a problem for you?"

"Sometimes, yes. My dad would never even hurt a fly, but there are occasions when I can explode into a rage. In the past, I've seriously hurt people and yet I don't really like fighting. I prefer to be helping people."

"You come from a tribe of warriors," said the woman slowly. "And you were a warrior for the devil. But now that God is turning your life around you will be a warrior for him, but not in a violent way."

When she said this, it instantly made sense. He

knew that in countries such as Sierra Leone, where his birth parents came from, witchcraft was often a powerful force, and that it was possible that somewhere in his ancestry one of his family had been involved in it.

On Friday night, while he was on his rounds, he stopped off at the Hope pub in Ilford. As he approached the entrance he saw that two blokes were arguing with one of his door supervisors. As he got nearer, he could see that the smaller bloke was slipping his belt off.

"Listen, mate," said Es, standing behind him.

The bloke spun round. "What?"

"It's not worth it. There's CCTV cameras here. Think about it." As he spoke to him, Es gently guided him away from the entrance to the other side of the road in front of an electrical shop. Es chatted with him, and after about twenty minutes he shook Es's hand and walked away.

The next morning, an acquaintance phoned. "Es, I heard about the bit of trouble last night. I hear that you pulled a gun on the bloke."

"A gun? Who told you that?"

"Someone in the pub."

"It's nonsense. My days of carrying guns are behind me," said Es, wondering if he would ever shake off his past reputation.

Following a difference of opinion, Es and Louis decided to split. Louis had been losing interest in the business. It saddened Es, as they had been a good team and seen the business become very successful over the ten years they had worked together, but he realised that there was nothing for it but to run WK on his own.

Es was learning that Satan was very active in the world. Before becoming a Christian, he would have laughed at any talk about the devil. How real Satan was came home to him one night when he was visiting a woman on a council estate in Dagenham. She was a Christian and had asked him to come and talk to her about understanding the Bible.

"Shall we pray?" asked Es, standing up and closing his eyes.

"Jesus is Lord," he began.

The woman stood up, but remained silent.

Es repeated, "Jesus is Lord."

Again she didn't respond.

"Who is Lord?" asked Es.

He opened his eyes to see the woman standing there with a wild look in her eyes, which seemed to be bulging. She then let out a roar in a deep man's voice, "Naaaah!"

"Jesus Christ is Lord," said Es firmly and loudly, and he began quoting Scripture.

The woman looked as if she wanted to grasp his shoulders, but couldn't. Es could feel himself sweating and his body suddenly felt weak.

"I break your power in Jesus' name," he shouted, a terrible fear gripping him. "In the name of Jesus, go! In the name of Jesus!"

The woman then let out another horrible roar: "Yaaaaagh!"

"In the name of Jesus, I bind you and rebuke you and drive you out," he called out loudly.

Suddenly she went limp and sat down on a chair. Breathing a deep sigh of relief, Es sat down in an armchair opposite her. But the woman then released another roar: "Naaaaah!"

"You spirit of death, leave in the name of Jesus!" called out Es.

The woman's expression returned to normal. "Es, I didn't want to hurt you," she said, looking up at him.

"Don't worry. I know it wasn't you. It was a demon." In the past, Es had been in some terrifying situations, but they were nothing compared to what he had witnessed with this woman.

* * *

Deciding he wanted to work in close protection, Es undertook a two-day induction course in Surrey and then went on a seven-day intermediate course at a training camp near the Brecon Beacons in Wales, run by ex-SAS soldiers. It was one of the most gruelling weeks of his life. At the end of the course, he was pleased to be told that he had come third out of twenty-nine, and that he had got top marks for fitness. But he was disappointed that he got a low mark in the firearms test. Following a further two-day course in Liverpool and a firearms course in Wales, he flew out to Marion, Alabama, USA, to undertake further training with Berkeley & Associates, who ran Ground Zero, a training centre which included sniper ranges, moving target ranges, a killing house, vehicle ranges and classrooms.

It wasn't long before Es began to get offered close protection jobs. He accompanied a guy to a car auction and a Jewish boy to his Bar Mitzvah, and then landed more high-profile work, accompanying Malcolm Rifkind from a theatre in Sussex to his home in London, and publicist Max Clifford from his office to a speaking engagement in the West End. He also had to organise a four-man team to provide protection for an Arab businessman who was attending a case in the High Court.

One day he was asked to collect a Mr Mason from the RAF Club and take him to Buckingham Palace. Es arrived at the club in a Lexus LS400 and went inside, straightening his tie as he did so. Mr Mason was waiting for him at reception.

"So it's the Palace, is it, Mr Mason?" said Es, opening the door for him while glancing up and down the street.

"Yes, that's right. I'm going to receive the MBE."

"I see. You must be important then," said Es, putting his sunglasses on and pulling out into the West End traffic.

Mr Mason smiled. "Well, I don't know about that, but I was Ambassador to Holland for a while."

At the gates to the Palace, the Old Bill closely examined the ID of Es and Mr Mason, and then waved them through.

"You can come in with me if you like," said Mr Mason, getting out of the car in a courtyard in the middle of the Palace.

"Er, I'll wait here if that's okay," replied Es, looking with interest at the armed royal protection officers standing around. He chuckled to himself and thought, 'If only my mum and dad could see me now. One minute I'm working the door in a spit-and-sawdust pub and now I'm moving among royalty.'

Es rented a unit on an industrial estate in Rainham, Essex, and began running training courses in close protection. He covered subjects such as enbussing, debussing, searching vehicles, disarming techniques and moving through buildings undetected. He also provided firearms training, but only with wooden guns.

One day, at a pub in Custom House, where he was the relief manager, he was chatting with Paul Armer, the guy who had trained him at the Havelock. Looking up he saw a big black bloke standing behind him. 'This looks like trouble,' he thought, tensing.

"You don't remember me, do you?" said the guy in a dead-pan voice.

"Nah, mate," replied Es, shaking his head and inching his chair towards the table to give himself room if he needed to defend himself.

"Snoopy," the guy said.

"Snoopy? Yeah."

"Plaistow Station."

"Plaistow Station? I know where it is." What was he talking about?

"You met me there. Snoopy sent me."

Then he remembered. "Yeah. What's up?"

"Snoopy's still in Spain. He runs a bar there now. He wants to come back to London, but he's worried what you might do if you meet him."

Es grinned. "Well, tell him I'm a born-again Christian now. Tell Snoopy I've forgiven him and he can come home."

Es demonstrating the use of the AR-15 weapon on a
Special Weapons And Tactics (SWAT)
course in Alabama.

Es in Mexico, training local students in
'High-risk VIP protection'.

Chapter Nine

Gunned Down

"So what do you reckon?" Es asked Andy Pohl when he walked into the office in Highams Park one morning.

"Doesn't seem to be too bad from what I can make out," replied Andy, perching himself on the edge of the desk. "Although they've got a late licence until 3 am."

"How many do we need?"

"Four or five. That should do it. The guv'nor told me that they've been having trouble with drug dealers and that the Old Bill will close them down unless they hire a reputable door firm."

Andy, Es's operations manager, had been to assess The Joiners Arms in Bethnal Green.

"Okay, I'll draw up an order acknowledgement," said Es.

Peter Corke then walked in. At twenty-one, he was Es's youngest door supervisor. He worked as a car mechanic for the Old Bill. Es had been impressed by the maturity he had shown during his shifts.

"How are things, Peter?" asked Es, reaching for the envelope containing Peter's wages.

"Fine, Es," he said brightly.

"Still enjoying the work?" he asked, handing him the envelope.

"Yeah. You know what, I was saying to my dad the other day that this is the best job I've ever done."

"Well, you're a good doorman, mate. I'm glad you like the work."

The owner of The Joiners Arms phoned in to say that he only wanted to pay for two door staff. Es said that he needed four or five doormen. The owner was adamant that he only wanted two. On Friday night Es put two men on the doors. Halfway through the night one of them was hit over the head with a bottle when he tried to eject a punter. The owner had said that there would only be 150 punters there, but there had been far more. This wasn't the first time Es had been given a misleading picture about a pub. The following Monday morning Es and Andy visited the pub, which was set among take-aways, scruffy-looking shops and mini-cab companies on Hackney Road.

"Listen, you told us that there would only be about 150 people in the pub on Friday. There was double that," Es explained to the owner.

"Well, I didn't expect that many to turn up," he muttered nonchalantly from behind the bar.

"Well, we're either going to have a team of seven doormen or we're not taking the job," said Es in a no-

nonsense voice, knowing that the owner wouldn't agree to a team of seven, but figuring he might agree to five.

The owner thought for a moment. "I ain't having seven bouncers. No way. You'll have to do the job with five."

The following Friday night, Es asked some of his 'early doors' staff, who usually knocked off at 11.30 pm, to go on to The Joiners Arms afterwards. Given that one of his team had been bottled, he was worried that trouble might kick off again. The rule was that everyone had to be searched before they were allowed into the pub. Some punters refused to be searched, claiming to be friends of the owner. The owner then let them in, much to the annoyance of Es's doormen. Over the next three weeks things improved a little at The Joiners Arms, but Es's team told him that there always seemed to be an undercurrent of trouble.

One Friday around midnight Es stopped off during his rounds. He made his way through the crowds of drinkers to Andy Pohl, who was standing by the toilets.

"How's things going, mate?" Es asked, scanning the pub.

"Okay, but we're warning people about using drugs," he said. "There's two brothers here who claim they run the manor. I've had to have words with one of them and I told him that if I catch him taking drugs again he's out."

"Okay, mate."

Just then, the toilet door opened and a bloke in a leather jacket came and stood between Es and Andy. Because of the loud music, Es couldn't tell what he was saying, but from the way he was wagging his finger at Andy he could tell that trouble was brewing. The bloke then turned and started making his way through the crowd, with Andy behind him. Sensing something was about to kick off, Es followed them. He then heard shouting and swearing from somewhere. Turning around, he saw a big guy in an Arsenal football shirt violently pushing and shoving his way through the crowd towards Andy. Es intercepted him by sticking out his left arm. Spinning round, the guy knocked Es's arm away. Es then grabbed him around the neck.

"Aagh! Get off!" he yelled, trying to get free. "Get off. That's my brother."

"Calm down, mate. If you calm down, I'll loosen my grip," said Es, keeping a tight grip on him.

"Okay! Okay!"

Es loosened his grip, but still kept the guy in a head-lock. The punters around him backed away. Es saw that the bloke in the leather jacket was waving a knife at Andy. Andy was too quick for him and managed to put him in a wrist-lock, but he couldn't knock the knife out of his hand, so he put one arm around the guy's neck and dragged him out of the pub. Still keeping the big bloke in a head-lock, Es led him towards the door. Outside, he saw the guy in the leather jacket lying crumpled on the floor, blood oozing from his mouth, with Andy standing over him. Punters started to spill out of the pub to see what was happening. Seeing the guy on the floor oozing blood, some girls started screaming and shouting. Several of Es's 'early doors' then appeared, followed by the owner.

"You're animals," a woman in a mini-skirt screamed at Andy.

Es watched the owner and four guys walk off down the road towards a blue car.

"Right, let's all go back in. We've still got a job to do," Es said to his team.

Es went and stood by a fruit machine, feeling anxious that more trouble could kick off. The owner then walked up to him and casually said through gritted teeth, "I'm going to do you."

"Come on then. Let's see what you can do," replied Es, staring him straight in the eye.

"Nah. Nah," he said, suddenly backing down.

"Listen, don't you threaten me. You might think you are Charlie big bananas, and you might well be Charlie big bananas, but I'm not bothered."

"Let's go and have a talk outside," the owner suggested, his tone changing.

"Okay," said Es, warily following him towards the door.

Unbeknown to Es, Peter Corke and another doorman, who were 'early doors', had followed him outside, standing a few feet away. As Es and the owner were talking, a shot rang out into the night air – then another. Es threw himself to the floor. More shots rang out. He lay there, motionless. Then he heard the voice of one of his doormen: "Es! Are you all right?"

'The gunman must have gone,' Es thought to himself. Picking himself up, he saw Peter Corke lying on the floor in a pool of blood.

"What's happened?" shouted Es, not knowing what to do.

"Some geezer appeared on the opposite side of the road and then started firing!" exclaimed a doorman.

"Call an ambulance!" screamed Es, crouching down alongside Peter. "Can you hear me, mate? Are you okay?" But Peter didn't move. His eyes were transfixed in terror and his mouth was wide open.

Es and three other doormen jumped into Es's van and sped off in search of the gunman. As the streets would be deserted, there was just a chance, Es felt, that they might find him. After driving around the dimly lit back streets for a while, they returned to the pub. Hackney Road had been cordoned off by the Old Bill, who were everywhere.

"Let me through," demanded Es, getting out of the van.

"Sorry. You can't come through. There's been a murder," said a young copper.

"What? He's dead?"

The copper nodded. "Why? Did you know him?"

"Yeah. He worked for me."

The following morning, Es returned to the pub to take part in a police reconstruction. When he saw the bullet holes in the wall, he was amazed. Had he not hit the deck when he did, then he would have almost certainly been killed. When he got home he had a bath and felt a painful stinging in his left shoulder. Looking in the mirror, he discovered that he had an indentation in it. A bullet had grazed him.

Hundreds of people turned up for Peter's funeral at the City of London Cemetery in Manor Park. Standing with the mourners, Es felt partly responsible for Peter's death and angry with himself for taking on The Joiners Arms.

He decided to quit the security business. Later that week, he decided to go and see Peter's parents at their home in Chadwell Heath to express his sorrow.

"It's not your fault," said Mrs Corke, pouring him a cup of tea. "Don't blame yourself, Es."

"I'm going to pack up this business. It's not worth anyone losing their life," said Es, finding himself staring at the photographs of Peter dotted around the living room.

"No, Es, you're doing a good job. Keep going," encouraged Mrs Corke.

Mr Corke nodded in agreement.

Es was surprised at her words. "You think so?"

"Yes. You're trying to do the job the right way. Don't blame yourself for Peter's death. It wasn't your fault. He loved working on the doors and was so grateful to you for giving him a chance."

After leaving Mr and Mrs Corke, Es drove to north Woolwich and parked his car near the ferry terminal.

A chill wind made him shudder as he gazed at the dark and brooding Thames and at the twinkling lights of Woolwich across the water. The sky was metal grey. Apart from the sound of cars and lorries going on and off the Woolwich ferry, which drifted backwards and forwards, the night was quiet. He thought about Mrs Corke's words. Maybe he should stay in the security business, after all. He knew that his job was to protect innocent punters on a night out. Eventually, he walked slowly back to his car, still unsure about what he should do.

How violent a world he moved in was further underlined when, just before Christmas, as he was driving across Tower Bridge, he heard on Capital Radio that three known drug dealers, Tony Tucker, who also ran a door firm and whom he had once met, Pat Tate and Craig Rolfe, had been found riddled with bullets in a Range Rover parked on a remote farm track in Rettendon, Essex.

The Old Bill eventually arrested a man for the murder of Peter. It turned out that they had found traces of gunpowder in the glove compartment of his car. Es felt that there was strong evidence against the guy. A doorman who was studying art in his spare time had provided an artist's impression of the gunman, who looked very much like the man who had been charged. However, at the trial at Southwark Crown Court the jury found the man not guilty. Es was stunned when he heard the verdict, as he felt convinced that the Old Bill had the right man. He left the court feeling deflated and depressed.

A few weeks later, he came home to find an eerie silence in his house in Abridge. He noticed that the children's coats were not hanging in the hall where they usually were and that their toys had gone from the living room. He ran upstairs to his and Carron's bedroom. The wardrobe doors were open and items of clothing were scattered across the floor. He checked the children's bedrooms and discovered the same scene. Going back downstairs, he checked the kitchen for a note. There was nothing. He went back into the living room and slumped down on the settee. Feeling distraught, he drove straight away to see Tony Sapiano and his wife Maria at their house in Redbridge. Tony was a builder who had become a Christian after serving a prison sentence for armed robbery. He and Es had first met at Elim Way Fellowship.

"Tony, I don't know what to do. I don't know where she's gone."

"She'll be back, Es. Don't worry."

Es shook his head. "No, I don't think she will this time. What am I going to do?"

"Let's pray about it, Es," said Tony, leaning forward and joining his hands. "Put your trust in God. She'll probably come back. She's done it before, hasn't she?"

"Yeah, she has. But something tells me that this is for good, Tony."

Carron didn't come back. Es didn't know where she had gone with the children – she had simply disappeared. Her mother claimed that even she didn't know where Carron was. Es began visiting Tony and Maria regularly for support. Often the three of them would pray together and Tony would reassure him that things would eventually work out. But every time he looked at the photographs of the children and saw their empty bedrooms, he felt that his world had fallen apart. The next few months were a miserable time for him. Some days he felt so depressed that he found it hard to summon the enthusiasm to go to work. His only consolation was in prayer and reading the Bible.

One night in October 1996, he was working on the doors at the Rat and Carrot, a busy pub opposite Ilford nick, when he met Rachael, whom he had known briefly while working at Crews back in the late 1980s. A few days before, she had phoned him and said that she would like to see him again.

"Where've you been hiding all these years, Es?" she said with a smile.

"Oh, here and there," replied Es.

"So how are you doing?"

"Fine. I've become a Christian."

She laughed. "Yeah, I'd heard from John the Kickboxer that you'd become a Bible-basher."

"I don't bash it. I read it," Es replied. "It's a good book. Tell me, Rachael, what's your heart's desire?"

"My heart's desire? Well, I suppose a good husband, children and a nice home."

They met the following week for lunch at Es's house and chatted about the old days and various people they both knew. Es played her a tape of him being interviewed on Premier Christian Radio, talking about his past and his faith. After it had finished, she said, "I'm pleased for you, Es, but Christianity's not for me."

Es felt the Holy Spirit telling him to ask her about her feet. He dismissed the thought from his mind, but it kept returning. Eventually, he said, "Rachael, how are your feet?"

Rachael was taken aback. "What do you mean?"

"How are they?"

"Well, three months ago I had an ingrowing toenail and I had to have an operation."

"Does your foot still hurt?"

"Yeah, it does today."

"Well, let me pray for you. The Lord will heal you."

"Pray? I don't know about that, Es," she replied awkwardly. Then standing up she added quickly, "Listen, I'd better get back to work."

As if dealing with the break-up of his marriage and the loss of his children wasn't bad enough, Es received a phone call one cold evening in November to say that his mum had died. He sat alone in the living room of the empty house that night, feeling numb and unable to even pray.

Es hadn't expected to hear from Rachael again, so he was surprised when she phoned and asked if they could meet. They went for a drink at a pub near Theydon Bois station and went back to Es's house afterwards.

"I've got a pain in my neck," she said. "Es, you can pray with me if you want to. I asked a mate who is a Christian if you were in a cult or something and she explained that Christians often pray for people."

"Okay," said Es, "I'm going to place my hands over your neck and ask God to heal you."

As Es prayed over her, she began swaying and then fell back onto the floor. She lay there for forty-five minutes. When she got up, she discovered that the pain in her neck had gone.

"Okay, Rachael?"

"Wow. That was incredible!" she smiled. "I felt a heat go through my body. What happened?"

"You've just had an encounter with God."

She shook her head in disbelief. "I've never experienced anything like that in my life."

"You were arrested by the Holy Spirit so that God could heal you."

A couple of weeks later, they met one Sunday afternoon near the Renault showroom in Ilford where Rachael worked in the office. They sat in Rachael's car. "I feel my life's in a mess," she sobbed. "I feel miserable." She told him that she was living with a guy and they weren't getting on. His brother was a drug dealer and she admitted to smoking cannabis regularly.

"Listen, Rachael, we all fall short. Just invite Jesus into your life and God will give you a new start. Imagine a book in which all the pages are ripped out and replaced by blank ones. That's what it's like when you ask Jesus into your life. But it's your decision."

She nodded. "I want Jesus in my life."

"Say these words after me, Rachael," said Es, closing his eyes. He then recited a prayer of repentance.

Rachael repeated the words. Afterwards, she couldn't stop smiling. "I feel great, Es," she beamed.

"Praise the Lord," chuckled Es.

Matthew Thomas came to see Es. A few months before, when WK were asked to run the doors at the Central pub in East Ham, which was popular with some of the ICF, Matthew had warned them not to cause any trouble with the door staff. He had been greeted like a hero when he had walked into the pub.

"Es, I'm in trouble," he said, sitting down in the kitchen. He went on to explain that he had been working on the doors at a pub in Dagenham and had got into a fight with a punter. The bloke had died and he was now on the run from the Old Bill.

"I need to borrow a car for a few days, Es."

Es didn't know what to say. Now that he was a Christian he had distanced himself from his past. On the other hand, he had known Matthew for thirteen years and he had been a good friend. But he didn't want to break the law. What would Jesus do in this situation? In the end, he decided out of loyalty and friendship to help Matthew. He couldn't lend him his Lexus, as it had been fitted with a tracker as a precaution against it being cloned by car thieves. When Rachael turned up he asked her if Matthew could borrow her Renault Clio. She agreed.

"Well, good luck, mate," Es said as Matthew got up to leave.

"Cheers, Es. I'll bring the car back tomorrow."

Afterwards, Es was troubled. He wondered if he had done the right thing. Matthew was a mate who had come to him for help and he couldn't turn him away, he concluded. Matthew returned the car the next day, as promised. Es didn't ask any questions.

*   *   *

Es and Rachael were married at East Ham Baptist Church on 14th April 1998. His best man was Kevin Wood, one of his operations managers, who had become a good friend. Among the guests were Andy Pohl, John Whitman, Lee White, who had become a Christian and was now a youth pastor at a church in the East End, and Alan Mortlock, the boxing promoter, who paid for the white Rolls Royce that Rachael arrived in. Soon after, they moved into her mum's house in Barkingside. Her mum had cancer and had gone to stay with her older sister in Basildon. A few months later, they moved to a house in Chigwell.

Es closed the office in Highams Park and rented a larger premises in a quiet residential street in Forest Gate. He now had a room that could be used for the door supervisor courses he was running. Up until now, he had been using the gyms and Alan Mortlock's snooker club in Chingford. WK had become an approved trainer of door staff for Westminster City Council. Local authorities were now demanding that door staff at venues in their area complete a recognised course in door supervision that covered subjects such as basic first aid; fire-fighting skills and evacuation; criminal, civil and licensing law; restraint techniques; and customer care.

WK were now supplying staff to around twenty venues, including Chimes nightclub on Lower Clapton Road, known as 'murder mile' because of the number of shootings that had taken place there, and Kursaal entertainment centre in Southend-on-Sea, as well as Gap shops, unlicensed boxing shows and even fairgrounds. Es was delighted to get the contract to supply door staff to several Latin American bars in the West End and Fulham. The contract was going well until he was told by Jeff, who had become his operations manager after Andy Pohl quit the company following the murder of Peter Corke, that the company was terminating it.

"You serious? Why?" he asked.

"Their area manageress reckons that the report from one of the West End bars wasn't very good," said Jeff, looking perplexed.

Each venue WK supplied was given a client liaison form to fill in. This asked them to comment on things such as the punctuality, appearance and overall performance of his door staff. He had introduced this in order to maintain high standards among his staff. Taking the reports on the Latin American bars out of the filing cabinet, he read through them. Overall, they were very good. Puzzled, he decided to put feelers out to see why the company had decided to end the contract. He was told by someone that the owner of another security company had got very friendly with the manageress of one of the bars and persuaded her to submit a bad report, so that he could get the contract himself. Es was fuming when he heard this. This guy had taken a right liberty. Part of him wanted a confrontation, but another part said 'no', because he might end up doing something he might regret. Es joined his hands, bowed his head and prayed, "Lord, you've seen what this bloke has done and you know it's not right. I've got to let you sort this one out because if I do it my way things will go wrong."

Ever since the time John the Kickboxer had tried to make a move on his doors he had been very vigilant about revealing too much information about the contracts with venues. One day, he discovered that Kevin Wood, one of his office staff – and the best man at his wedding – had passed on confidential information on the company to another security firm. When Es heard this, he was furious. He drove to Fairlop Waters, where the man was working on the doors. Es was amazed to see that he was wearing a tracksuit and trainers instead of a black suit.

"What you doing dressed like that?" demanded Es.

"Stacey said that she doesn't mind," Kevin replied.

"You don't work for Stacey; you work for me. It's for

Stacey to tell me how she wants her door run. Can I have a word upstairs?" said Es tersely, trying to control his anger. They went into the empty function room.

"What's the problem?" Kevin asked casually.

"Now, listen. I know what your game is. I know about the information you've given to that other firm."

"Don't know what you're talking about, Es," he lied.

"You know exactly what I'm talking about. I trusted you when I took you on, and now you are going behind my back to another outfit. That's it. Finished." With that, Es turned to walk out. As he did so, he saw Kevin smirking. This habit had always annoyed him.

"So you think it's funny, do you? Well, I'm not laughing," Es said, exploding and punching him hard in the face. Kevin collapsed as if in slow motion onto the floor.

'What have I done?' thought Es, standing over him. 'I'm supposed to be a Christian.' Panicking, he quickly left, got into his van and immediately phoned Rachael. "Rachael, I think I've just killed Kevin Wood!" He then explained what had happened. "I didn't mean to hurt him. Pray that God raises him from the dead."

When he got home, he and Rachael began praying that Kevin wouldn't die. Es felt he had let God down. As they finished, Es's mobile phone rang.

It was Jeff. "Es, Stacey's just rang me and she says you've beaten Kevin up. He's in hospital."

"Praise God!" said Es, closing his eyes.

Kevin recovered and he didn't press charges. This incident reminded Es yet again how difficult, at times, he was finding it to live as a Christian in the security business.

Scouse Pete (centre) at his wedding,
flanked on left by Louis Whittaker
(Es's partner in WK) and Es on right.

Chapter Ten

On Fire

As the prison came into view, Es felt a kind of chill run through him. Not for the first time, he realised that he too could have ended up behind walls like these if he had carried on living a life of violence. "There but for the grace of God go I," he prayed silently as he parked the car beside the visitors' centre.

"A bit anxious, Es?" asked Benny Stafford.

"No, just thinking that I probably would have been sent down if Jesus hadn't entered into my life, Benny."

"Yeah, mate. You might well have done. I've been inside, as you know, and it ain't no hotel, I can tell you."

It was a bright Sunday morning and Es had joined Benny, George Strange and Reg Gardener as part of the prison ministry team at the Elim Way Fellowship in Canning Town. They were visiting Blundeston, a category C prison housing over 450 prisoners in Lowestoft, Norfolk. When Benny had suggested to Es about getting involved in prison outreach, he wasn't sure he wanted to do it, even though he had visited several prisons with Alan Mortlock and Ian McDowell. Given that the outreach work took place at weekends, when he often didn't get home from working the doors until the early hours, he wondered whether he could make a commitment to it. However, over the next couple of weeks he prayed about it and felt that God was calling him to go and talk with prisoners.

Benny had been a well-known boxer and villain, and had been instrumental in bringing Jimmy Tibbs, a member of the infamous Tibbs family, who ruled Canning Town in the 1960s, to Jesus. Following a ten-year prison sentence in 1972, he had gone on to train boxers such as Frank Bruno and Nigel Benn, who both became world champions. George, a former merchant seaman and docker, had found Jesus while serving a prison sentence for fraudulent trading and running a factory that manufactured amphetamine sulphate (speed). Reg was a former car salesman and market trader who used to drive around the East End in a Rolls Royce. Once, halfway through a karaoke night in a pub in Canning Town, he took the microphone and began telling people about Jesus.

As soon as Es walked into the prison, he felt a coldness and a sadness engulf him. It was overpowering. He could hear shouting and banging from the wings. Bill Salmon, the Anglican chaplain, met them in the reception and then took them to his office, unlocking and locking doors as he went.

"I don't know how many we'll get today. You never

can tell. We might get thirty or we might get sixty," he said, switching the kettle on.

"I know," said Benny. "We'll leave it to the Lord."

"And, Es," continued Bill, "you probably know that you can't ask the men what they are in for. If they want to tell you, it's up to them."

"Yeah, I understand," Es replied.

The chapel, which was on the top floor, was quite light and airy. At one end stood a lectern, and a simple wooden cross adorned the wall. Es was surprised to see a drum kit and two guitars at the front. He looked at the bars on the windows and silently prayed, "Lord, thank you for keeping me out of prison." Then the inmates began to file in, looking with curiosity at the team before taking their seats in the first few rows. Bill introduced the team and then picked up a guitar and launched into an upbeat hymn. After it finished, he invited the inmates to offer any prayers out loud. A few did so, but most remained silent. He then said, "Now, I'm going to introduce Es, and he is going to tell you how the Lord changed his life."

Es stepped forward, prayed for the Holy Spirit's inspiration, and then began to talk about how he had become a Christian. When he reached the end of his story, he paused and then said, "Remember that Jesus was the friend of sinners and he accepted people who were rejected by the world. And if he can change my life, he can change yours as well."

After George and Reg had given their testimony, tea, coffee and biscuits were served at the back of the chapel. A tall, lean guy covered in tattoos wandered up to Es and said, "Thanks for sharing that, mate. It was powerful stuff."

"Yeah, the Lord has worked miracles in my life. But don't forget something," replied Es, pleased that the guy had been listening to him.

"What?"

"I'm not perfect. I still fail in my life. Without the grace of God I'm nothing."

The guy then explained that he had been a professional boxer and had been convicted of murder. "I know what I did was wrong. I took a life. But I believe in Jesus and I've committed my life to him."

Impressed by the guy's honesty, Es said he would pray for him. After lunch in the restaurant at the local Tesco, the team returned to the prison in the afternoon for a second session, where inmates could ask questions about God and Christianity. Driving back down the A12 to London, Es felt glad that he had decided to undertake the prison ministry. What these men needed above anything was hope. He began visiting the prison with the team every six weeks.

During one visit, a Greek guy from the East End came up to him in the chapel and said, "Drugs have brought me a lot of money, but I've caused misery."

"Yeah, that's the truth, mate. Jesus said in John's gospel that while the devil comes to kill, steal and destroy, he has come that we might have life and have it more abundantly. Listen, mate, many of us have caused misery to other people. I know I did. Being honest with God is the first hurdle if you want to change."

"Yeah, I do. I regret what I've done and how I've hurt others."

"Well, there's hope. You are showing remorse for what you've done. But you need to pray."

"I don't know how to."

"Just pray in your own words."

Es gave him a Bible and each time he went back to the prison he prayed with him. Eventually, he did become a Christian.

Another time, a big black guy who had been convicted of drug dealing said, "I want to give my life to God, but there's something stopping me."

"You will never be ready," Es replied. "The Bible says that all fall short of the standard that God sets for mankind. It's by God's grace and through faith that we are saved. One of the men crucified alongside Jesus was a thief. But he acknowledged his sins and Jesus promised him eternal life."

"We'll talk again when you come next time," said the guy.

"Okay. But don't give up," Es encouraged.

One morning, Es drove to Swaleside prison on the Isle of Sheppey to visit Matthew Thomas, who had been convicted of threats to kill, false imprisonment, perverting the course of justice and using noxious substances. Es had intended to visit him sooner, but he was worried that if he was known to associate with him it might have a detrimental effect on his business. But when he asked himself what Jesus would do, he knew he should go and see him.

"How are things going?" asked Es, sitting down in the visiting room.

"Okay, Es," he replied, trying to be cheerful.

"I'm involved in prison ministry now, Matt."

"Yeah?"

"I go to a prison in Norfolk with some blokes from the church in Canning Town."

"Well, I believe in God," said Matthew.

"But are you born again?"

"I don't know about being born again, but I believe in God in my own way."

"I'll pray for you, mate."

Matthew brightened. "Cheers, Es."

While stuck in a traffic jam just before the Dartford Tunnel on his way back to London, Es reflected how God works in different ways with people. Matthew might not be born again, but who could say that God was not active in his life?

*　*　*

A phone call one summer evening in 2000 found Es sitting in the living room reading his Bible.

"Hello, Esmond. How are you?" said the voice at the other end. It was the chief instructor at Berkeley & Associates in Marion, Alabama.

"Fine. What's up?" asked Es, wondering why he had

phoned. He had done a number of special weapons and tactics courses with Berkeley & Associates. He had felt so proud when he had been awarded his diploma as a senior instructor a few months before, for he had not forgotten how, as a child, he had seen black people in Alabama on TV marching for their rights and being attacked by federal troops. Here he was now, a black man who was qualified to teach white men skills in law enforcement.

The chief instructor then explained that a group of former KGB and special forces officers were coming over from Russia the next day for a week-long special weapons and tactics training course. He was concerned for the safety of one of his instructors, an English guy, who had been dubbed 'the Mafia buster' because he trained Russian law enforcement organisations in how to deal with organised crime. He knew that a contract had been put out on the English guy and that one of the Russians on the course might have been paid by the Mafia to kill him by faking an accident.

"Can you come over immediately and provide some close protection for him? I want you because I can trust you and you are good at your job."

"Yeah, I'll come straight away," he said, feeling both flattered and a little anxious, because he knew that he would have to be armed. As a Christian, he did not want to have to shoot anyone, but he was prepared to do this if someone's life was in danger. If a situation arose where he had to pull the trigger, he would aim for the shoulder or arm of the person holding a gun to disable them. He would only shoot to kill as a last resort. When he told Rachael about the trip, she said "Es, be careful out there."

"Don't worry, love. God will protect me," he said, trying to reassure her.

Rachel then helped him pack. He took two black suits, black SWAT T-shirts, armour vest, Magnum boots, revolver holsters and torches, and the following day flew out to Newark Airport. From there, he caught a connecting flight to Birmingham, Alabama, where he was met by a car from Berkeley & Associates. The driver told him that the FBI would be watching the Russians.

Arriving at the training centre, he was briefed on his mission by the chief instructor and also asked to help out with the training. He was then issued with his 9mm semi-automatic pistol. He booked into the same nearby motel where the seventeen Russians were staying. Among them was Alex, a surly man with killer's eyes who, he learned, had been the personal bodyguard to President Gorbachev.

Throughout the week, Es never let the English training instructor out of his sight. The course went smoothly until the Russians refused to carry out an exercise often known as a step and drag retreat, a technique for remaining in a combat crouch while retreating safely. The idea is to move slowly backwards, using your right foot to feel for anything behind you, while never taking your eye or gun off the target, in case you need to engage. But the Russians stayed standing upright and ran backwards instead. Es knew that in a real-life situation if there was a kerb or something else behind them, they would fall over. When he explained to them through the interpreter the reason for step and drag, he could see from the expressions on their faces that this made sense. Alex, however, seemed unimpressed. He whispered something in Russian and the rest of the group began laughing. Angry, Es said to the interpreter, "Tell him I don't care who he is or what he's done, but if he doesn't do as he's told I'll shut the range down." This would mean that the course would also have to close and they would return to Russia in disgrace.

Alex's smile disappeared when he heard this. "Okay. We'll do it," he muttered in Russian, fixing Es with a menacing glare.

Looking at him, Es could tell that his pride had been hurt, so from then on, Es made sure he was always alert, in case the Russian tried anything. Alex hadn't become Gorbachev's bodyguard for nothing. He stayed in what's called condition one, with his gun cocked and locked, at all times, even when he was in the motel. The rest of the week passed off without incident. During the flight back to London, Es felt drained by the week in Alabama and yet he felt a sense of satisfaction in completing the mission successfully.

Es now supplied staff to pubs and clubs in London, Essex, Kent and Buckinghamshire, and his son Carl worked for him as field manager. Es had been steadily raising the professional standards of his company, renamed Grace Services. He maintained the name WK for his training division. He had moved his business from Forest Gate to a village near Chigwell, where he and Rachael now lived. He had felt the move would be more economical and, because it was in the country, provide the staff with a more pleasant working environment. Also, as he and Rachael now had two children, Jessie and Pearl, it would mean that he could be around more.

Es had set up a Wednesday evening prayer meeting to attract the type of men who would never set foot in a church. He figured that a low-key meeting, where they could talk about what was going on in their lives and speak honestly to God, might appeal to them. He was right. Some well-known faces had started to come along. He called it the Market Place, because Jesus went into the market place to meet people.

For some people, Es felt, a nightclub became a sort of church. This was where they came in search of some kind of experience that would lift them out of the mundane nature of day-to-day life. Through loud music, flashing lights and an endless supply of alcohol, clubs created an illusion for a few hours. But when people went home in the early hours, the look of expectation they had had when they arrived had disappeared, and they would wake up the next morning feeling empty. To deal with this emptiness, increasing numbers of people were now turning to drugs. When Es was offered a contract at a pub or a club he would make it clear to the management that he wouldn't tolerate the sale or taking of drugs on the premises. He would say, "If I catch anyone taking drugs on the premises, they go out the door. I'm protecting your licence. If I allow drug taking, you're going to get undercover police coming to the club and you're going to attract major drug dealers coming to sell their gear. And with them you'll get fights and shootings."

If he discovered that the management were allowing drugs to be dealt at a venue he would terminate the contract. He would have nothing to do with drugs because of the misery they caused in people's lives. It was through drugs that Peter Corke had been shot dead at The Joiners Arms. However, he had been in the business long enough to know that it was quite likely that some of the venues he supplied staff to were turning a blind eye to drug dealing.

One evening at Kites nightclub in Southgate, north London, Es was searching a young guy at the entrance.

"Woops, mate, be careful," said the guy when Es crouched down and ran his hand down his right leg.

Es looked at him, his suspicions aroused. "Why, what's the matter, mate? You got something there?"

The guy shook his head. "Nah. I've got arthritis in my leg and it's painful."

"Yeah? Well, listen. Jesus can heal you."

"You what?"

"Jesus can heal you. Do you want me to pray for you?"

Some of the other punters in the queue were laughing nervously at this scene. The last thing they had expected was to see a bouncer offering to pray with someone.

"Okay," replied the young guy uncertainly.

Remaining in a crouched position, Es placed his hands on his knee and prayed in a low voice. Afterwards, the guy shook his hand and went into the club. At the end of the night, when the club had been cleared and all the staff and management were having a drink, the DJ pointed at Es and said, "See him. He healed my mate. He had arthritis when he came in and when he left, it had gone."

"No, it wasn't me, mate. It was Jesus who did it," corrected Es, aware that everyone was looking at him.

* * *

Es drove down to Dartford in Kent in order to meet the management of Jay's nightclub to discuss security arrangements. While in the town, he took the opportunity to pop into the Litten Tree, a large, busy pub, where he supplied door staff. The pub was run by Pete Edwards, a friend from his days at the Ilford Palais. Walking in, Es saw Tracey, one of the staff, sitting at the bar. "How you doing, Tracey?" he asked.

"Not too great. I've got another hospital visit. Hopefully, it will be okay," she replied, then added, "touch wood."

"What's that lump of wood going to do for you?"

"What do you mean?"

"You're putting your trust in a lump of wood. That's

dead. I put my trust in God, who is alive. So what's the matter with you?"

"The doctors say that I have a collapsed back. I find it difficult to bend over."

"Jesus can heal your back."

She gave a hollow laugh. "What?"

"I'm not joking. Speak to Nina." Nina was a Finnish barmaid who had attended one of Es's Wednesday night prayer meetings and asked everyone there to pray for a friend back home to be cured of cancer. And she was. Tracey called Nina over and she explained how her friend had gone to the hospital soon after the prayer meeting to be told by the doctors that they could find no sign of her cancer.

"Let me pray for you. The Lord's going to do something for you, and when he does don't put it down to me, to coincidence, to self-healing or any-thing else. It's going to be down to Jesus," said Es.

"Okay," said Tracey.

The three of them went upstairs to the staffroom. Es placed his hand on Tracey's head and began to pray. She began to sway.

"Okay, Tracey, see if you can bend forwards," he said.

Slowly, Tracey bent forwards. "My back feels all right," she said after a few moments, her face brightening.

"Praise God!" exclaimed Es. "Thank you, Jesus, for what you've done for Tracey. And Tracey?"

"What?"

"Remember: Jesus is alive. If he wasn't, you wouldn't be healed."

Tracey was speechless.

Soon after, Es was having a drink with the staff at Jays nightclub at the end of the evening when a barmaid said, "If there's a God, why do good people die? And what about children?"

"I don't know the answers to everything, but in the Bible you can often find the answers. We are all born to die."

"Yes, but what about children?" she repeated.

"In the Bible it says that the sins of the forefathers will revisit the children. I can commit a sin today and it will travel down my ancestral line. I believe this has happened in my case." He then told her about the counselling he'd had.

"Well, that's not fair," she said.

"Course it's fair, because God told us through his word. People often say, 'What goes around comes around.' This comes from the Bible, where St Paul says that whatsoever a man sows, that he shall reap. This is what the Bible means when it talks about the sins of the fathers."

The barmaid nodded thoughtfully. "I see."

"Well, I'm not into religion," said a barman.

"Jesus isn't about religion. He wants a relationship with us, whoever we are and whatever we may have done. That's why he sat down with the prostitutes, publicans, cut-throats and gangsters of his day."

The discussion continued for some time. Afterwards, as Es was putting the two-way radios, hand-held metal detectors and earpieces into the boot of his car, he felt that he might have got some of the staff thinking a bit more about God; that he might have sown the seeds of faith.

*   *   *

Just before Christmas, promoter Alan Mortlock invited Es and Rachael to an unlicensed boxing show and dinner at the Prince Regent Hotel in Chigwell. Es was enjoying this rare night out when he didn't have to be on duty. After the boxing was over, a fight broke out on the dance floor between Steve, a well-known local drug dealer, and Terry, a boxer. Terry was pounding the drug dealer mercilessly. Grabbing Terry tightly in a bear hug, Es pulled him off. "That's enough! That's enough!"

"He was making fun of my brother!" Terry said breathlessly, swearing at Steve, who was lying on the floor.

"Okay, mate, but leave it now."

Es and another bloke picked up Steve and sat him on a chair at a table.

"Come outside with me to cool off," said Es to Terry.

The two of them made their way outside to the forecourt of the hotel. As Es was talking to him, a bottle flew past, missing his head by inches, and smashed against the wall, splattering the back of his cream suit with red wine. He spun around to see Steve disappearing through the foyer. Fuming, Es went back into the hotel and made his way to the bar. Spotting

Steve sitting in the corner with his mates and a couple of girls, he went over to him.

"Listen, I was trying to save your bacon. You owe me a new suit," he said firmly.

Steve smirked back and then suddenly stood up, slipping his hand in his trouser pocket as he did.

Knowing that he was rumoured to carry a knife, Es tensed. "Leave that where it is," he warned.

Steve stared back at him. He hesitated and looked worried. Then he walked off, followed by his mates and the girls. Es looked round to see Roy Shaw, the former bare knuckle fighter and still a legend in east London, and Alan Mortlock standing behind him.

"I didn't know what was happening, mate. Then Rachael came up to me at the bar, so Roy and I thought we'd better back you up," said Alan.

"Cheers, Al," replied Es, thankful for their intervention.

A few days later, Es received a phone call telling him that the drug dealer had left £300 for him at a gym to buy a new suit.

* * *

Es was given the contract to run the door at Club One9Five, tucked away in a narrow lane in the centre of Epping, a small town in Essex and the last stop on the Central Line. The club had become a popular venue, especially with local faces, professional footballers, pop stars, actors and models. He hadn't been there long when a well-known East End face with a fearsome reputation turned up, dressed in an immaculate suit, decked in gold jewellery. With him were several other blokes, all well built and smartly dressed.

"Good evening," said Es. "I've just got to search you before you go in."

"What do you mean, search me?" replied the face indignantly.

"I'm sorry, sir, I have to search you." Es was hoping the guy wasn't going to kick off, but he couldn't have two different sets of rules.

The man studied Es for a moment and then lifted up his hands. Es ran the hand-held metal detector up and down him and then said, "Thank you. Enjoy the evening, sir."

"No problem, mate," the man replied, walking on. His mates then obediently lined up to be searched.

At the end of the night, the face came up to Es. Es tensed slightly. Was he going to start something?

"You're doing a good job here, mate," said the face, extending his hand.

"Cheers," said Es, taken aback.

Another time, David Hunt, a member of a well-known East End family whom Es had first met while working at Roxanne's in Stratford many years before, arrived at the club on a Sunday night for a ticket only event.

"Look, Es, my boy is with me," he said, motioning to his car parked in the High Street. "He's not on the guest list and he doesn't have a ticket, but I wondered if there was any way he could come in tonight. If it's going to cause you a problem, don't worry about it."

"No, he's all right," said Es, impressed by how respectful he was.

"You sure?"

"Yeah, no problem, David."

"Cheers, Es," he said, signalling to his son in the car.

Another figure from the old days, Vic Dark, phoned Es one day. He had since served time in prison for an attempted armed robbery at the Penthouse in Ilford, during which he shot the owner and also, accidentally, his accomplice.

"How you doing, Es?" asked Vic cheerily.

"Not bad, Vic. Good to hear from you."

"So what you been up to?"

"I'm a born-again Christian," replied Es.

"You are, are you?"

"Yeah, given my life to the Lord, Vic."

"Well, good on you. I was banged up with a born-again, Christian but it's not for me, Es."

Putting the phone down, Es resolved to pray that Vic would find faith in Jesus. He reminded himself that God was patient. While Vic had a genuine reputation, there were others who were wanabees. One night, Es was talking to a local businessman at the top of the stairs at Club One9Five when one of the bar staff called him. He went into the bar and saw a bloke with curly hair arguing with several of his doormen. A couple of weeks before, Es had refused him entry because he had turned up at the club wearing trainers.

"What's the problem?" asked Es.

"One of your doormen swore at my mate," growled the curly bloke.

"Oh yeah? Which one was that?"

"Him," he replied, pointing to Lee, Es's nephew.

Es knew that Lee never swore. He was one of the politest and most respectful doormen he employed. "It didn't happen," he said flatly.

"What?"

"It didn't happen. I know this lad – in fact he's blood," said Es firmly. He had used the word 'blood' because he knew that it was a term this guy understood.

The curly bloke looked at his mate, a tall guy with a big nose and beady eyes. "Did he swear at you?"

"Yeah, he did."

Es could see that the curly bloke was looking for a way out. Es fixed a fierce gaze on the mate. "I'm telling you, mate, it didn't happen. I know him. He doesn't use that kind of language."

"Did he swear?" the bloke asked his mate again, only this time more timidly.

"Er, I thought he did," murmured the other guy.

The curly bloke muttered something and he and his mate moved away to the other end of the bar. But Es knew that he would have to watch him carefully. He could see that his pride had been dinted, and this was often a trigger for trouble.

Not long after, Es saw the same bloke arguing with

several of his doormen. Angry, he went over and stood between them. "That's right. Yeah, yeah," said Es impatiently.

The bloke swore under his breath and walked off. A short while later, he came up to Es with some of his mates standing behind him. Es gave him a look that said, "Do your best. The talking's done." The last thing he wanted was a tear-up with the bloke, but his patience had run out.

"Let's go," said one of his mates, moving towards the exit.

The curly bloke hesitated and then turned and sheepishly followed. Afterwards, one of the owners of the club came up to Es and said, "Es, you frightened me then."

"I don't like anyone taking liberties," replied Es. "I might be a Christian, but I ain't a mug."

That night when he got home, Es replayed the events in his mind and realised how close he had come to losing it. But he had managed to control his anger – something that he would have found impossible a few years before. He prayed for self-control because he knew only too well that without the grace of God he was powerless.

* * *

In April 2004, Es went with Rachael, some friends and doormen to the Showcase cinema in Beckton to see the Mel Gibson film *The Passion of the Christ*. Sitting there, he felt disturbed and stunned by this graphic and controversial portrayal of Jesus' last twelve hours.

"What's the matter, Es?" asked Rachael when they came out of the cinema.

Es stopped and said, "You know, Rachael, watching that film made me realise even more what Jesus did for me on the cross."

"I know what you mean," she nodded.

They drove back home to Chigwell in silence, both still thinking about the film.

Two or three days later, Es was standing at the door to Club One9Five, directing male customers to Jason to be searched and female customers to Faye, who had worked for WK for eleven years and had been one of Es's most loyal staff. Faye remarked that she had also been to see *The Passion*. "It was a brilliant film," she enthused. "I didn't really know much about Jesus. But why did he die on the cross, Es?"

"To explain this I would have to take you back to the beginning with Adam and Eve. Eve nagged Adam to take the forbidden fruit. The serpent then came up to him and said, 'If you don't eat from the tree of knowledge, how will you know anything?' They listened to the voice of the serpent rather than the voice of God. From that moment, we were separated from God. God decided to send himself in the form of flesh: Jesus."

Every time there was a lull in customers, both Faye and Jason would ask him more questions. Es tried to answer them as simply as possible.

"Why did God send himself in the form of a human being?" asked Jason.

"Because God knew that we needed to be able to identify with someone like us. Jesus was like us in everything but sin. He was the new Adam, the perfect man."

"I need a sort of idiot's Bible," Faye giggled.

"I'll get you a copy of *The Message*," said Es.

"What's that?"

"It's a paraphrased version of the Bible in modern English. It's dead easy to read."

"Okay. Sounds interesting."

*   *   *

Despite his active faith, Es's past is never far away. He was driving to Guildhall University to discuss security arrangements for a student event, when his mobile rang and there was a familiar voice at the end of it. It was Joe, a well-known criminal from north-east England.

"Es, how you doing?"

"Fine, Joe. I haven't heard from you in ages. So what you up to nowadays?"

"Oh, this and that," he replied cryptically. "Listen, I wondered if you could do a bit of work for me."

"What?" Es guessed what was coming.

"There's a bloke in Reading who owes a mate forty grand. Can you help him get it? There'll be a cut for you."

"Yeah, I can help. Tell your mate to phone me. I run

a licensed debt collecting agency now."

"Licensed? That's not what I was talking about."

"I'm legit now, Joe. If he wants me to help him I will, but only in the legal way."

As Es expected, Joe never phoned him back.

* * *

Since shadowing actor Leslie Grantham all those years ago at the Palais, one of the perks for Es has been to meet a number of celebrities. He was asked to provide security for the birthday party of actor Gary Lucy, star of *Footballer's Wives*, at the Sunborn Yacht Hotel, a modern luxury ship berthed in Royal Victoria Dock. *OK* magazine organised the party and numerous celebrities turned up, including Katie Price – better known as Jordan – and stars from *Hollyoaks* and *EastEnders*.

There is also an ongoing self-examination, as Es recently explained during a meal at the Harvester pub in Woodford with Alan Mortlock, where they were discussing security for another unlicensed boxing show.

"Don't you ever think of turning your back on this game, Es? I mean, there are easier ways of making a living," said Alan.

"Yeah, there have been times when I've thought about packing it all up. I'll be honest, it's hard to keep your cool with some of the people you deal with."

"So, what keeps you in it?"

"I feel this is where God wants me to be, Al. With all the hassles you get running the doors, it would be very easy to leave it all and do a job that wasn't as stressful."

"I know what you mean, mate," smiled Alan.

"As you know, Al, I was left for dead when I was attacked at the Palais all those years ago. But each time I've prayed about it, I've felt God telling me to carry on because he wants me to reach people that the church can't – just like you in the unlicensed boxing world. It's a calling, not a job. Yeah, God doesn't like a lot of the things that go on in pubs and clubs, because we're his children and he doesn't want us to harm ourselves. It's just like us with our kids. He hates the sin, but he loves the sinner."

Es with his son Carl, who has joined him in
the security business – and in the faith.

In the USA, anti-terrorist training.

Epilogue

There are many people, I suspect, who find the idea of a Christian running a company that supplies bouncers or, as they are now called, door supervisors to pubs and nightclubs surprising. So I decided to put a few questions to Es when I met him one afternoon at his office in Chigwell.

A Bible lies open on his desk. Next to it is a batch of purple flyers for a champagne/cocktail reception at Club One9Five and a venue log, listing any incidents that took place during a shift. A large coloured poster depicting the anatomy of the human body hangs on one wall. On another, attached to a clipboard, is a list of pubs, clubs and venues Grace Services supply door supervisors to, along with the staff contact details. On a white board, near the PC and printer, are the words 'Men's prayer breakfast 8 am.' On the floor in the corner is a black bag containing hand-held scanners, two-way radios and earpieces.

GW: Some people might find it hard to understand how you can be a Christian and also work as a doorman. What would you say to them?

EK: If I didn't think it was God's will, then I wouldn't do it. I always pray, "Lord, if this is not your will, shut the door" – no pun intended –"because I don't want to do this work if you don't want me to do it." I've asked the Lord for Scripture passages to confirm that I'm doing the right thing. He has shown me Psalm 144:1–2 "Praise be to the Lord my Rock, who trains my hands for war, my fingers for battle. He is my loving God and my fortress, my stronghold and my deliverer, my shield in whom I take refuge, who subdues peoples under me." I believe there's a reason why God wants me to do the work.

GW: What do you think that reason is?

EK: I think he wants me to be in the security business so that I can speak about him to the people I work with and meet. If Jesus was walking the earth today, I believe that he'd go into pubs and nightclubs, because that's where many people meet. He was a market-place man who mixed with tax collectors and prostitutes. Before I set off for work I always pray that Jesus will provide opportunities for me to speak to people so that they will come to know him. I also pray for the safety of not just all my team that night but also the management, staff and customers.

GW: What is your approach when it comes to talking

about Christianity to people you meet?

EK: If I asked people to come to church, they would probably tell me where to get off. I talk about Jesus to people and tell them what he did for me. And I say to people that I'm special to God and so are they. I know that many people think that Christianity is irrelevant. I used to think this. I had a skewed image of Christianity and God, but I now know that Christianity is not about going to church and going through various rituals. It's about Jesus of Nazareth and his message of new life through faith. The Mel Gibson film The Passion of the Christ shows how Jesus suffered for us and how much he loves us.

GW: And if you are talking to someone whom you know to be involved in crime?

EK: As I've shortcomings and weaknesses, I allow for the shortcomings and weaknesses of others. I understand where people are coming from. I don't judge anyone. But equally I don't endorse criminal activity. I was a sinner saved by the grace of God. According to the Pharisees I should be locked in prison with the key thrown away. But God sees beyond our pain and hurt. He can see the goodness in us. Jesus loved me so much that he healed me, and he not only healed me but he also gave me the gift of eternal life. He gave his life for me, a scumbag. He will forgive us, no matter what we have done, but there are conditions. We have to acknowledge that he died for us and come to him in a spirit of openness and repentance.

GW: How do you maintain your Christian principles in an environment which is often characterised by violence, drugs and organised crime?

EK: It's true that certain pubs and nightclubs have a reputation for being linked to violence, drugs and crime. I know a number of faces and London families and they know that I'm a Christian. I can't honestly say how they all view me, but I think many respect me for being prepared to try and live out what I believe to be true. And they know that although I'm a Christian, I'm not a mug. Since becoming a Christian, there have been some occasions on the door when my temper has got the better of me, I admit. But, as time has gone on, I've learned to control it. I've only been able to do this through the power of Jesus.

GW: But what about using violence?

EK: As a doorman there are times when I have to use physical force to deal with someone who is causing trouble. But this is controlled. True, I'll defend myself if I'm attacked. We all have a right to self-defence. People probably think of door work in terms of physical strength, but in fact most of the work is psychological. It's about knowing how to read people and situations. You learn to pay particular attention to body language, especially as the combination of loud music and alcohol makes conversation very difficult. In the old days if I hit someone, I might have stamped on their head or squirted them with ammonia. I'd never do that now – I'd only use the amount of force necessary. I see being a doorman as similar to being a police officer or a soldier. I couldn't do this work without the Holy Spirit. I can honestly say that in ten years I've only ever used my hands four or five times. I always try to keep the atmosphere light when customers arrive at a venue. I'll often say, "Enjoy the evening." If I see a large group of guys, I might say something like, "Have a great night and enjoy yourselves. We want to see you again." I'll say this in a voice that is friendly but also firm. When I'm patrolling a pub or club, I never walk with a swagger, like some door supervisors. Instead I walk with my head high but also nodding and smiling to people. My message is, "This is my club tonight and you are welcome if you behave yourself."

GW: Have 9/11 and other terrorist attacks, such as the bombing of the club in Bali, affected the way you handle security at nightclubs in London?
EK: Not really. Nightclubs, like any other place where large numbers of people gather, could be a target. But we haven't stepped up security in any way. We are always vigilant to potential risks to customers.

GW: And what about your attitude to drug dealing in pubs and clubs?
EK: Drugs drive a lot of crime today. If I wanted, I could sit back in my office and make a fortune by giving dealers permission to sell their gear where I run the door. It was through drugs that Peter Corke got

shot dead in September 1995. The guv'nor of the pub was behind the dealing. My own son, Carl, got into drugs at one time. Thankfully, he saw how they were wrecking his life and he stopped taking them. He's now a Christian. If I find out that the management are allowing drugs to be dealt, I'll pull my guys out. The job is dangerous enough without this. Dealers send runners out with a bag of drugs and they're expected to come back with a wedge. If they don't, the consequences might be fatal for them. The guv'nors at one club I know in south London are scared of a local firm, so they allow them to deal drugs. Our doors are clean.

GW: How does God speak to you?
EK: Sometimes he can speak through the Bible and other times through people or incidents. When Marcus invited me to Kensington Temple, I now know that it was God speaking, not him. I didn't know this at the time, though.

GW: What about prayer?
EK: Prayer is the way we communicate with God – it's as vital to life as eating or drinking. As I told John Whitman that time we stood in the yard of the disused unit next to Fort Galaxy gym, you can pray anywhere: in a pub, on the bus, the train, in the car, at work. God says in Philippians 4:6, "Don't worry about anything, but in all your prayers ask God for what you need, always asking him with a thankful heart."

GW: Do you believe in miracles?

EK: Miracles are not just something that happened in the Bible. I've witnessed God bring about miracles in people's lives. I can think of Tracey, who was cured of an enlarged heart; Maureen of cancer of the lung; Don of sciatica; Jackie of multiple sclerosis; Nicky of infertility (she now has four children); and Mark of a deformity just to name but a few people. My own healing was a miracle. Not just my physical injuries but also my emotional and mental state. How did the preacher know so much about me? He'd never met me before.

GW: What about the devil?

EK: The devil is very real, as I witnessed that time with that woman in Dagenham. Many people may laugh at the idea of the devil today, but there is a spiritual warfare taking place in the world between good and evil, and we need to put on the armour of God. St Paul says in Ephesians 6:12–18, "For we are not fighting against human beings but against the wicked spiritual forces in the heavenly world, the rulers, authorities, and cosmic powers of this dark age. So put on God's armour now! Then when the evil day comes, you will be able to resist the enemy's attacks; and after fighting to the end, you will still hold your ground. So stand ready, with truth as a belt tight round your waist, with righteousness as your breastplate, and as your shoes the readiness to announce the Good News of peace. At all times carry faith as a shield; for with it you will be able to put out all the burning arrows shot by the Evil One. And accept salvation as a helmet, and the word of God as the sword which the Spirit gives you. Do all this in prayer, asking for God's help."

GW: So how do you look back at your days before you found God?

EK: All I wanted to do was to protect people. Although I wasn't averse to having a punch up, I didn't want to deliberately hurt people. A lot of the rucks I got into, such as that time at the Ealing night-club, were on behalf of someone else. But even before I was a Christian there were certain things I wouldn't get involved in, such as drug dealing and prostitution. I'd never picked up a Bible and I knew nothing about Jesus, but I had a moral code, which I think I'd picked up from my mum and dad. But I know that there were situations where I hurt people, such as when I hit that bloke on my first night working at Fairlop Waters, and thought I'd killed him. When one of my doormen said that I could team up with some other firms and run organised crime in London, I was tempted. It was the power that drew me. If I'd have followed his suggestion, I'd have probably ended up doing a life sentence in prison. Or six feet under – like one of my ex-doormen who was shot dead at the Frog and Nightgown on the Old Kent Road in south-east London. Reflecting on that night at the Palais when those blokes viciously attacked me, I thank God for it. That might seem a strange thing to say, but if I hadn't received that beating, I'd never have come to God. That incident could have resulted in me taking revenge by arranging for those blokes to receive a severe beating – or even worse. But because I forgave them, I had an encounter with God and my life was transformed.

GW: As a black man, how has being adopted by a white couple affected your life?
EK: If I'd not had the love of my adopted parents, then I might well have grown up with a chip on my shoulder about being black in Britain. I could have developed a very warped attitude to white people, especially after that beating in the back of the police van and I might have ended up doing a long stretch in prison.

GW: How do you square being married three times with being a Christian?
EK: None of us are perfect. In life, it's easy to make wrong choices that seem right at the time. I'm at peace with God over this and I thank him for the seven wonderful children I have.

GW: How do you think people should deal with their weaknesses?
EK: The first step is to acknowledge your weakness, whether it's an addiction, your temper, pride or whatever. My temper has been one of my weaknesses. When I realised this I sought help through Christian

counselling and had a lot of prayer. God revealed through the counselling the root of my problem, and that brought release and freedom. In 2 Corinthians 12:9, God says, "My grace is all you need, for my power is strongest when you are weak."

GW: How important is forgiveness?
EK: One of the hardest things to do is to forgive someone who has hurt you. I know that from my own life. It's not easy living as a Christian because at the heart of the message of Jesus is that we must forgive. If we can't forgive, it causes a blockage in our life. When we do forgive, it clears away this blockage, and it's often a path to healing. Also, and just as importantly, we have to learn how to forgive ourselves. This can sometimes be harder than forgiving someone else. One of my favourite passages in the Bible is Mark 11:22–25 when Jesus says, "Have faith in God. I assure you that whoever tells this hill to get up and throw itself in the sea and does not doubt in his heart, but believes what he says will happen, it will be done for him. For this reason I tell you: When you pray and ask for something, believe that you have already received it, and you will be given whatever you ask for. And when you stand and pray, forgive anything you may have against anyone, so that your Father in heaven will forgive the wrongs you have done."

GW: So what would you suggest to someone who wants God to enter their life?

EK: I would say, first of all, acknowledge God and that Jesus came into the world and died for each one of us. Then confess your sins, repent of your sins and ask Jesus to come into your life. He will forgive you and you will be filled with the Holy Spirit. Say this short prayer of repentance: "Father, I come to you in Jesus' name. Father, I acknowledge and believe that you sent your Son to die for me, as well as all mankind. He died for me so that I could be forgiven of all my sins. I confess all my sin and renounce the devil. I want to be a new creation in Christ Jesus. I want to be born again, filled with your Spirit. Come, Holy Spirit, fill me now in Jesus' name. Amen."